Haiku
Utah

Haunted Utah

Ghosts and Strange Phenomena of the Beehive State

Andy Weeks

Illustrations by Marc Radle

STACKPOLE BOOKS

This one is for my mom, Vivian
Thank you

Published by
STACKPOLE BOOKS
5067 Ritter Road
Mechanicsburg, PA 17055
www.stackpolebooks.com

Printed in the United States of America

10 9 8 7 6 5 4 3 2

FIRST EDITION

Cover design by Tessa Sweigert

Library of Congress Cataloging-in-Publication Data

Weeks, Andy.
   Haunted Utah : ghosts and strange phenomena of the beehive state / Andy Weeks ; Illustrations by Marc Radle. — 1st ed.
      p. cm.
   Includes bibliographical references.
   ISBN 978-0-8117-0052-8 (pbk.)
   1. Ghosts—Utah. 2. Haunted places—Utah. I. Title.
   BF1472.U6W436 2012
   133.109792—dc23
         2012004049

Contents

Contents

Introduction

WHEN BRIGHAM YOUNG LED A BAND OF MORMONS TO THE SALT LAKE Valley in the summer of 1847, he spoke words that have been immortalized by Utahans ever since: "This is the right place." Since that hot July day more than a century and a half ago, Utah has become known as "the place" of rugged mountains, pristine rivers, awesome lakes, desert landscapes, wide streets, neat communities, and a number of ghosts and haunted hot spots.

It's true that you don't have to search far to find stories about ghosts and strange phenomena in the Beehive State. Though one of the union's younger members, the state is rich in folklore, urban legend, and people who claim they personally have experienced things that can only be described in the context of the paranormal. The area's religious heritage might explain, at least in part, Utah's haunted history.

Utah was admitted to the union on January 4, 1896, as the forty-fifth state. For at least two thousand years before statehood, however, the Ute Indians had spread across the Colorado Plateau, many of them living in the shade of the Rocky Mountains. Some bands lived in the bulbous mountains in the northeast portion of what is now Utah, thriving off the rich sources of game and fish, while other bands eked out a living in the arid deserts to the west and south. Pristine landscapes, developed only by the campfire or wigwam, stretched far and wide until the pioneers arrived in 1847 and Mormon communities began to rise.

The Mormons, fleeing persecution in the Midwest, had left the United States and sought sanctuary in Mexican Territory (later Utah

Territory). Years before they entered the Great Salt Lake Valley, church founder Joseph Smith claimed to have seen in a vision the great migration of the Latter-day Saints and their arrival in the Rocky Mountains. Smith, however, never saw in person their new Zion. In 1844, three years before the Mormons entered the valley, Smith was struck down by a mob's bullets in Carthage, Illinois. It was his successor, Brigham Young, who fulfilled Smith's prediction, leading thousands of Latter-day Saints to their promised land.

Young and his company arrived on July 24, 1847. Stopping at the mouth of what today is known as Emigration Canyon, Young, who lay in the back of a wagon because of an illness, looked over the fertile valley and proclaimed, "It is enough. This is the right place. Drive on."

Once here, Young directed church members to spread out, sending some north and south to colonize and establish communities rich in agriculture and faith. Their efforts didn't sit well with the Ute Indians and other tribes, who had lived here for centuries unmolested. Their only contact with the white man before the pioneers arrived was with the occasional fur trapper or explorer. Relations with Mormons and Indians often were contentious, as were the relations between the Mormons and federal government.

The Latter-day Saints, nicknamed the Mormons because of their belief in the Book of Mormon, called their home Deseret, a name taken from their sacred book that means "honeybee" and symbolizes industry. But others, years later when statehood was imminent, petitioned for the name Utah, which in the Ute vernacular means "Top of the Mountains." In a show of goodwill, it was nicknamed the Beehive State.

The Mormons proved to be industrious indeed, for here they built businesses, welfare centers, wide streets, thriving communities, churches, and a magnificent temple that Mormons believe, in part, fulfills a prophecy by the Old Testament prophet Isaiah: "And it shall come to pass in the last days, that the mountain of the Lord's house shall be established in the top of the mountains, and shall be exalted above the hills; and all nations shall flow unto it." (Isaiah 2:2.)

For many people the words "Mormon" and "Utah" are synonymous terms, but that need not be the case. Utah is a state that over the years has become more diverse in both its population and its religions. According to 2010 population estimates, nearly three million people, both Mormon and non-Mormon alike, called Utah their home. It's true, however, that you cannot understand Utah history without knowing something of the Mormons, because of the religion's influence in the state's settlement, growth, and development. Much of Utah's population today resides along the Wasatch Front, in urban sprawl that stretches from Ogden to Provo's Utah Valley. The mix of big cities, small townships, farming communities, open space, and outdoor venues attracts a number of new residents every year, both the religious and secular. In 2002, Utah attracted the world's attention when it played host to the winter Olympics and Paralympics. And in early 2009, Utah was voted as one of the country's best places to live. "Here residents reported a high level of satisfaction in several areas, including work environment, emotional health and their local communities," reads a March 2009 article in *Forbes* magazine.

And what of Utah's ghosts? There are plenty of them, according to the stories, some that have circulated for decades. And not only stories of ghosts, but monsters that allegedly inhabit lakes, strange creatures that have been seen wandering in residential communities, and unexplained lights in the skies. Some of these tales have survived since the Indians roamed the foothills, others have sprung up in more modern times. All of them are interesting and tell another part of Utah history—its colorful, haunted heritage.

Do you believe in ghosts? According to at least one public survey, the number of people who believe in some kind of paranormal activity is on the rise. Three in every four people believe in paranormal, according to a June 16, 2005, Gallup poll. Thirty-seven percent of responders say they believe houses can be haunted. (This number was slightly higher, forty percent, for Britons and lower, twenty-eight percent, for Canadians.) An interesting number, since thirty-two percent say they believe a dead person can come back from the Great Beyond to certain places and situations. The poll also found that thirty-one percent believe in telepathy, twenty-six percent in clairvoyance, twenty-one percent believe that people can communicate mentally with someone who has died, and twenty-one percent believe in witches. Extra-sensory perception or ESP received the most support at forty-one percent.

Five months later, in November of the same year, Gallup published a follow-up piece with additional information about its previous findings. "Women [forty-two percent] are more likely than men [thirty-one percent] to believe in haunted houses, communicating with the dead, and astrology," the poll reads. "Men, on the other hand, show a slightly greater proclivity than women to believe in extraterrestrial beings." There's even a group among the younger crowd who say they are believers in the paranormal. In a nationally representative survey of more than three thousand teenagers, for instance, many said they were open to believing in astrology, psychics, and communicating with the dead, according to the National Study of Youth and Religion.

What would such a poll reveal of Utah residents? It's difficult to tell since no poll currently is available. But I've encountered a number of people through the research and writing of this book who very much believe, some from personal experience, that things do go bump in the night. Also, a cursory search of the Internet reveals that a number of paranormal and ghost-hunting groups exist in the state, attesting that there must be a need for such groups. What's more, Utah has a strong religious history that produces people who believe in the afterlife. This also, of course, causes an argument.

How people view the afterlife varies from one person to the next and from faith to faith. Some Christians, for instance, regard the Bible's teachings about the afterlife as infallible: "And it is appointed unto men once to die," Paul wrote to the Hebrews, "but after this the judgment." (Hebrews 9:27.) Others, some who also profess belief in the Bible, possess a more liberal view. A journalist friend of mine reported this in an October 31, 2009, newspaper article: "As reality-TV programs such as *Ghost Hunters* or Discovery Channel's *Ghost Lab* continue to grow in popularity, concepts of the afterlife are moving into the realm of tangible documentation and other scientific theories, and there are those who find a balance. For them, the venture into the dark of night with a video camera and a flashlight could stand to affirm their faith that there is life after death."

What's your answer to the question? You're reading this book for a reason, so I assume it's either because you believe in the supernatural, or you simply like ghost stories. Either answer is fine by me. But even if you're a born-again skeptic who has other reasons for reading this, consider the following question: Why do some people like being scared? Why do they enjoy watching horror movies or reading Stephen King stories? Answer: Because believing in ghosts is fun. That's what I hope you experience from reading this book.

This book is not a definitive volume of Utah ghost stories, urban legends, and folklore. It is doubtful that one could even be written, for as paranormal writer and fellow Stackpole Books author Rosemary Ellen Guiley wrote in her book *Haunted Salem*, "we still know so little about ghosts." But these are the stories, some of them not shared in other publications, that caught my attention; the ones I thought you'd most enjoy reading. I hope you like them.

Northern Utah

WELCOME TO NORTHERN UTAH, WHERE THERE ARE WIDE-OPEN SPACES, large lakes, friendly people, and plenty of ghosts. Here you'll read about lake monsters, phantom horseback riders, an elegant but haunted hotel, Bigfoot sightings, and more than a few spirits—some friendly, others not so much.

Monsters in Bear Lake

You've heard of Nessie, the famous cryptid reputed to inhabit a particular lake in the Scottish Highlands. Tales of the Loch Ness Monster have circulated for decades, but years before the now-famous monster was brought to the world's attention in 1933, pioneer settlers heard about monsters in several Utah lakes. The most famous was the Bear Lake Monster. Rumors still circulate of a serpent-like creature that occasionally is seen in the cold waters of the resort lake.

The lake, nicknamed "The Caribbean of the Rockies," because of its white beaches and turquoise-colored water, has become a popular destination for outdoor enthusiasts who from near and far come to take advantage of its many attractions such as boating, camping, fishing, hiking, and off-road riding. Long before its current popularity, however, the lake and surrounding area was prime hunting grounds for the Indians because of its abundant supply of buffalo and black bear, from whence it received its name. As long as the Indians have known about the area's bears, there have been stories about a prehistoric monster that would rise out of the watery deep, spew water from its mouth, and carry away members of the tribes as they bathed near the shores.

Stories of the monster were told to the pioneers when they began to settle the valley in the 1860s and became popular after Joseph C. Rich wrote an article for the Mormon-owned *Deseret News*. The article, "Monsters in Bear Lake," appeared in the July 31, 1868, edition. Rich told about the Indian legend and then shared new tales about the water monster. It wasn't long after the article was published that the pioneers began rehashing their own encounters with what became known as the Bear Lake Monster. Before long, it was common knowledge that a strange, prehistoric creature lived in the lake. A man named C. M. Johnson, according to the book *Folklore in the Bear Lake Valley*, claimed he saw the head and long neck of a creature rise from the water's surface. Even Brigham Young seemed to have believed the stories, because he supposedly offered rope to a hunting expedition to snare the monster.

Stories about sea creatures that roam the expansive and often unexplored ocean depths are one thing, but how did a freshwater monster arrive in an inland lake? One assumption was that the creature, whatever it might be, was a prehistoric entity left over from Lake Bonneville, which existed thousands of years ago and covered one-third of Utah and parts of neighboring states. But according to geologists, Bear Lake is not a remnant of that ancient lake, but instead was created separately about twenty-eight thousand years ago. However the monster arrived, it apparently wasn't alone. In 1871, the *Salt Lake City Herald* reported that a man had captured a young member of the monster family near Fish Haven. "This latter-day wonder is said to be about twenty feet in length, with a mouth sufficiently large to swallow a man without any difficulty, and is propelled through the water by the action of its tail and legs."

Interestingly, twenty years after Rich's article was published, he confessed that he had made up the tales after he heard the Indian stories, hoping to attract attention to the area. Rich's confession didn't stop the stories from circulating, however, and more eyewitnesses reported seeing the strange water creature. Descriptions have varied, with witnesses claiming the monster resembled a walrus, large carp, dragon, crocodile, or duck-billed creature. It is said to be anywhere from twenty feet to ninety feet long and able to swim up to sixty miles per hour.

In recent years, a man named Brian Hirschi claimed to have seen the monster on an evening in June 2002 while sitting in his monster-shaped pontoon boat. Recounting the experience in a July 11, 2004, Associated Press article written more than two years after the incident, Hirschi, after throwing anchor, claimed to have seen "two humps in the water." He at first thought they were water skis, but was surprised when one of the humps caused his boat to be lifted up. "The next thing I knew, a serpent-like creature shot up out of the water," he said. He described it as "really dark" with "slimy green skin and deep beet-red eyes." When it again submerged it made a sound like "a roaring bull before taking off." People who heard or read the story believed that Hirschi, who owned several rental shops in the area, made up the tale to promote tourism in the valley, especially since the original article was published during Memorial Day weekend, start of the valley's tourist season. But Hirschi, according to the news article, said he debated on whether to circulate his story, fearing people would think him crazy. Despite his fear, he finally decided to share it.

What do you believe? Were Hirschi, a handful of pioneers, and the Indians savvy marketers or real eyewitnesses to a prehistoric water serpent? It's likely that, as with the Loch Ness Monster, most visitors to the lake will not see the Bear Lake Monster. But remember, not seeing it isn't a valid attestation that such a monster doesn't truly exists.

Little Girl Lost

It is an age-old question: Why do some spirits linger after death? Those who've studied the paranormal say ghosts are attracted to places that were either special to them in life or places where a traumatic event occurred, perhaps the place of their mortal passing. This begs the question about the Main Theater in the small town of Smithfield: What importance does the theater, built in 1899 and located at 141 North Main Avenue, have for the ghost of a little girl rumored to haunt there?

"It's a very unique building," said Kevin Erickson, director of the Cache Paranormal Research Society, whose group has conducted several investigations in the theater house-turned-concert venue. "We've had very good luck with getting a little girl's response in there." The group has recorded phantom voices and witnessed objects move. Others, according to local gossip, have reported hearing footsteps, ghostly laughter, doors slamming, and seeing apparitions.

One of the more memorable experiences of Erickson's group involved a girl's play doll. During one investigation in the building's projector room, where the girl's ghost seems to hang out, the group sought interaction by placing a doll on the floor. The doll was placed in a sitting position against a wall. For several minutes nothing happened, but as the group petitioned a response the doll began to move. "It slid about five or six inches across the floor and lied down," Erickson said.

Apparently this little lost ghost girl, believed to be around eight or nine in mortal years, is not the only phantom to haunt the theater. The shade of an adult male also allegedly has strange attractions to the place. But it is not known why he or even the ghost girl are attracted to the old movie building or who they might have been in their mortal lives. Though some people claim to feel a sense of foreboding when in the building, Erickson said he's never felt anything malevolent.

Today the building is used as a concert hall. Maybe there's a simple reason why the spirits reside here; perhaps it's because they like entertainment and the arts, attesting that there is good taste even after this life.

Haunts at an Old Indian School

Brigham City is a quiet, scenic area in northern Utah's Box Elder County. Known for its plentiful fruit groves, the city holds a Peach Days celebration every year around Labor Day. People come from all over the valley and, in some instances, farther away to participate in the parade and other activities hosted on these special days in community life. But like any place, the city has its darker side.

One dark spot, when viewed from the paranormal angle, is the Intermountain Indian School. The multi-building complex that sits on a seventeen-acre parcel near the foothills was formerly known as the Bushnell Army Hospital, which from 1942 to 1947 served wounded American servicemen and German, Italian, and Japanese prisoners of war. At the time, the site offered bowling alleys, a golf course, gymnasiums, a swimming pool, tennis courts, and a theater. After it closed as a hospital, Utah senator Arthur Watkins secured the site and Congress approved $3.75 million for remodeling. The goal was to open it as a federally funded Navajo boarding school in an effort to help fulfill the government's wish to better assimilate Native Americans into mainstream society. Providing schools where young Indians were taught basic English, math, and other academic skills was the government's way of doing this. The school opened in 1950 with around five hundred students, most coming from Arizona.

Enrollment numbers remained steady over the next two decades, but by the early 1970s cracks began to show in the government's well-intentioned—though far from concrete—plans. To encourage enrollment, the school refocused and changed its name to the Intermountain Inter-Tribal School, which then served students from nearly thirty different tribes. But it was doomed to failure. The school closed in 1984 after the federal government relinquished control. The site was deeded back to Brigham City, with the stipulation that it remain open space.

And there the school buildings sit, alone and lonely, except for the vandals, daredevils, and ghosts that haunt the complex. Because of its history as a hospital, it was likely the site of many deaths, giving credence as to why it might be haunted. The site also saw a lot of trauma, both from the hospital's patients and later from the school's emotionally strung students. Over the years people who've visited the place have claimed to have felt a chilling presence. It's not uncommon to hear stories about the eerie tunnel system built during World War II that serves as a meeting place where devil worshippers conduct their satanic rituals. It's reported that the walls are stained with blood from sacrifices made in the tunnels' dark, forbidding recesses. Apparitions, flying objects, and shadow people all have been reported at the old complex. These aren't just urban legends, said paranormal investigator Kevin Erickson. "A lot of things actually have been documented," he said. "There's been a lot of nasty stuff in there, a lot of satanic symbols, burned carcasses."

Police frequently patrol the old campus, trying to ward off trespassers.

Perhaps you have to be a little off your rocker to visit the place, because even without the ghosts the silence of the once-busy complex is haunting enough. If these buildings could talk, what would they say? Now owned by Utah State University, most of the buildings were slated for demolition in late 2011. Erickson said on July 16 of that year that he'd like to legally put his team of investigators on the grounds and was working toward that end. "Nobody has ever done an investigation in there legally . . . we want to be the first."

Only a few of the buildings are still in use, including one now used as a furniture store, where delivery men have reported seeing shadow figures and feeling unnerved.

Ghost Children at Crybaby Bridge

The woman felt a growing heat in the pit of her belly, her mind turning to darkness. Two children sat in the backseat, chatting away but sensing something wrong with their mother. The woman began to talk gibberish, saying things the children had not heard their mother say before. Their mother wasn't acting like herself. The children stopped chatting and now spoke in whispers and quiet sobs. What was wrong with their mother? they wondered. Their growing fear turned to utter dread when she recklessly and willfully pointed the car off the bridge, plummeting the family to a tragic end below. Or so the story goes.

A common American urban legend has to do with crybaby bridges, something many states seem to have. The stories associated with them usually are about the spirits of young children who, having died tragically at the bridge in question, often are heard crying out for their mothers; or the mothers are seen or heard looking for their lost babies. Utah's Crybaby Bridge is located in Bear River City, and similar to the other stories, it is one about a mother who, possessed by an evil spirit, steered the vehicle she was driving off the bridge with her two children inside. But like the eternal existence of spirits, the story doesn't end there.

Today when you drive across the bridge, roll down your window and honk your horn three times and you supposedly will hear the ghostly children cry out: "Don't do it, mother!" Of course, there's only one way to find out. If you're ever driving across the bridge, try honking your horn to see if the legend has any truth to it.

Ogden's Elegant Haunted Hotel

"Hotel rooms are a naturally creepy place," says John Cusack in the movie *1408*. Based on a Stephen King story, the movie tells about paranormal writer Mike Enslin, played by Cusack, who rents a room on the fourteenth floor—there is no thirteenth—of the magnificent Dolphin Hotel. Over the years, as the story goes, a number of people died in the room—some from natural causes, others from murder and suicide. Enslin, a skeptic because he has not experienced anything paranormal even though he writes about it, intends to stay in the room overnight, hoping to capture something ghostly. He gets more than he bargained for, and he doesn't even have to stay the whole night. The possessed room tries to kill him within the first hour of his stay.

Like all good fiction, the story contains nuggets of truth. If you've ever stayed in a hotel, for instance, you'll likely agree with Enslin's assessment: "How many people slept in that bed before you? How many of them were sick? How many of them lost their minds? How many of them—died?"

Though it doesn't have quite the reputation as the Dolphin, the Ben Lomond Hotel in Ogden shares enough similarities to the on-screen hotel that it's not too difficult to let our minds wonder what paranormal activity might take place behind closed doors. Such activity is rumored to occur on just about every floor of the Ben Lomond. Its history might explain why.

Built in 1927, the hotel replaced the smaller five-story Reed Hotel, which was built in 1891. It was believed at the time that Ogden, a popular stopping spot for train travelers passing through the Beehive State, needed a grand hotel and convention center. The hotel, first named the Bigelow, received its current name in 1933, when Marriner S. Eccles, a name familiar to Utahans, acquired the building, naming it after nearby Ben Lomond Peak. The building continued to change ownership over the years and today is owned by Radisson. It was listed in the National Register of Historic Places in 1990.

Despite its highbrow status, it has a few dark spots that allegedly give it its haunted history. The hotel, like most of the 25th Street area in downtown Ogden, especially in its early days, attracted both the famous and infamous. Some of the more thorny breeds who've left their dark mark on the city include drug smugglers, gamblers, murderers, and prostitutes. In his day, mafia warlord Al Capone allegedly visited Ogden and stayed at the Ben Lomond. One rumor, perhaps a bit humorous in hindsight, claims that once Capone left the city he said, "Ogden is too wild a town for me." But even the master criminal left his mark on the city. At least a few murders either committed or ordered by Capone are said to have taken place in the hotel's basement.

Today, if you visit the Ben Lomond, its pleasant staff will greet you with warm smiles. And a few folks, depending on their sensitivity to the paranormal, might feel, see, sense, or smell a resident ghost. Stories of the strange and paranormal abound about the Ben Lomond. It's likely that some of the stories have been made up, but probably not all of them have.

One of the more famous rumored stories of death is about a woman who drowned in the bathtub while staying in Room 1102 on her wedding night. Why she'd take her life on what was supposed to be a happy day for her is anyone's guess. Was it an accident? Murder? As urban legends often go, there is no explanation as to how she drowned. The story doesn't end there. Supposedly her son came to the hotel, distraught after hearing about his mother's death, and there in a room next door, took his own life so he could be with her again in the spirit realm. Both of the spirits are said to haunt their respective rooms.

The ghost of a World War II–era woman allegedly haunts Room 1106. As the story goes, she came from out of town and stayed at the Ben Lomond, waiting for the arrival of her soldier son, who was injured in the conflict. It turned into another unhappy ending: He never showed up, at least not alive. And the woman never left the hotel. She committed suicide, but her spirit lingers behind in the hotel room, still waiting for the arrival of her soldier boy.

Ghostly children have been rumored to haunt the narrow hallways on the fourth floor. The apparitions of playing children, their ghostly laughter echoing through the hallways, have been seen by more than one witness.

The Ben Lomond has been featured in a variety of ghost-hunting websites and other publications, including Francis Kermeen's *Ghostly Encounters: True Stories of America's Haunted Inns and Hotels*. Kermeen is best known for her popular book about Louisiana's Myrtles Plantation, dubbed America's most haunted house. In her book about haunted hotels, Kermeen includes a story about a former Ben Lomond staffer named Gerdi Curran. The hotel maid said she didn't believe in the ghost stories until she started working at the Ben Lomond. After she started working at the hotel, she felt chills, smelled phantom perfume, received strange phone calls, and more than once was pushed by an unseen force. "I don't like it when the ghosts push me," she says in Kermeen's book. "I haven't fallen down, but they push hard."

Some stories, such as the phone calls Curan received when cleaning a room—she'd answer it to find no one was on the other end of the line—might be explained away as a prank from a fellow worker. Others are more difficult to explain, such as smoke rumored to be seen on stairways that form into the shape of a woman. Other allegedly haunted rooms include 212 and 1010, the latter where visitors have reported seeing apparitions. Also, the hotel's elevator seems to have a mind of its own, often stopping on the fifth floor without any buttons being pushed.

Are these stories true or are they fanciful tales made up over the years to attract people's attention to Ogden's most grand hotel? Hotel manager Blake Citte said he's never seen or experienced anything paranormal at the hotel, nor has he felt any sense of dread or foreboding. He doesn't shun the notion of his hotel being haunted; he only claims he has not experienced anything unusual himself. Because of the long hours he puts in at his job, he feels the hotel has become a second home for him. "I'm more comfortable here than I am at home," he said.

The Phantom Train of Dove Creek

Life wasn't always as we know it today. As difficult as it might be for the younger generation to consider an existence without cell phones, iPods, and the Internet, there really was a time when those things were but the stuff of imagination. Likewise, at one time, so were super jets screaming across an azure sky or even the whistle of a steam-powered locomotive.

In their day, the builders of America's railroad system dreamed of a time when tracks would stretch across the heartland to the untamed West. The idea of a transcontinental railroad, in fact, had been dreamed of since about 1836. It became more than a dream once gold was discovered in 1849 in California. Four years later, in 1853, Congress passed an act providing for a survey of several lines from the Mississippi River to the Pacific Coast.

In Utah, the railroad workers, many of them Chinese immigrants, sweated under a desert sun to complete the arduous task. Injury and death were common fare for the workers, who blistered their hands for something that, from an industrial perspective, was bigger and more important than they.

Thanks to these workers, America's dream of connecting East with West—with the Union Pacific tracks joined to those of the Central Pacific Railroad—was realized on May 10, 1869, when the last spike was driven into the desert ground at Promontory, Utah. The joining of the tracks bridged more than two thousand miles and helped the western states to grow in commerce and population.

Like the builders of America's highways, railroad workers were a hardworking lot. And some of their spirits are still restless. One place the spirits of former railroad workers allegedly haunt is Dove Creek Camp in Kelton. Stories have circulated among paranormal groups, on websites, and in books about the ghostly shades, rattling noises, and phantom trains that make their appearance in this desert camp not far from Promontory.

Some people have claimed to have heard ghostly voices in Chinese dialects; others say that the clear, unmistakable sounds of footsteps have been heard in the area. On his website PrairieGhosts.com, popular paranormal writer Troy Taylor writes about Steve Ellis, a former park ranger who claimed to have seen the apparition of an old steam locomotive that headed toward him on the tracks. "He could see nothing but the small light of what appeared to be a lantern in the darkness. Frightened, he returned to his tent and retrieved his old rifle, trying to convince himself that nothing was going to hurt him. . . . Then he saw what appeared to be dozens of tiny lights, like sparks flying up from steel rails. The lights fluttered around him for a short time and then vanished."

When Ellison shared with others what he had witnessed, he learned that he wasn't the only one to have experienced strange happenings at the old Chinese camp. A number of people over the years said they also had heard strange noises including "the ghost locomotive which is said to still travel on the long vanished rails."

Sasquatch Sightings

For at least four centuries people have claimed to have seen hairy, manlike creatures stalking the forests of North America. Over the last two hundred years, since 1810 when David Thompson, a surveyor and trader, spotted large footprints resembling human feet near the Columbia River Gorge, the strange creatures, whatever they might be, have been known as Bigfoot. It wasn't until the 1930s, however, that the idea of Bigfoot became legendary in American culture, as sightings of the alleged beast began to be reported all over the country, from the Florida Everglades to the Pacific Northwest.

Modern technology has done little to dim the number of reported Bigfoot sightings. Between 2000 and 2010 there were sixty-three reported sightings in Utah alone, according to the Bigfoot Field Researchers Organization, a scientific research group that explores the mystery.

Bigfoot sightings have occurred across the state, but perhaps most especially in the High Uintas. "Only 10 of the 50 states have more reported sightings of 'Sasquatch' than Utah," wrote Lynn Arave in a September 30, 2003, article in the *Deseret News* titled "Utah Legends: Does Bigfoot Roam while Gold Lies Hidden under Indian Maiden?" Arave continued, "Many of these purported experiences are reported in or along the Wasatch Mountains. From the mountains east of Ogden and North Ogden to the foothills of South Weber and Francis Peak, sightings date back almost 25 years."

Utah's first major Bigfoot sighting occurred in late August 1977, when a group of campers—six boys and two leaders—reported seeing a creature similar to the classic Bigfoot description. Instead of brown fur, however, they claimed the creature had a "white mantle of hair over its shoulders and half-way down its huge body," which they estimated stood about ten feet tall, according to an article by

Bert Strand in the August 25, 1977 edition of the *Ogden Standard-Examiner*. Jay Barker, one of the witnesses, said the lower half of the creature was dark colored.

Barker said he had hunted big-game animals for years in the area and had never seen anything like what he came across on that late summer day when he was hiking with the group. The group watched the creature for several minutes as it stood by Fish Lake, about a half-mile away from where they were. It turned to look at them and then began to wander off into the woods, still turning its head from time to time to look at them. The group went to the area where they had seen the creature and found large "paw-like" imprints in the dirt. Reports of sightings by others soon followed, as well as reports of strange growling and howling sounds in the area. It wasn't long before a team of Bigfoot experts from around the country arrived in the Beehive State to look for the mysterious creature. Three weeks later, on September 15, 1977, the *Davis News Journal* reported that "scores of persons have scoured the high Unitas looking for the human-like monster" only to return with "nothing conclusive."

For at least one week in February 1980, people living in South Weber reported seeing a strange, hairy creature stalk their neighborhoods. Thoughts of the eyewitnesses immediately turned to the acclaimed legend of Bigfoot, a primate-like creature that over the years has been captured only in grainy photographs.

South Weber resident Pauline Markham claimed that on the afternoon of Sunday, February 3, 1980, she saw a tall, hairy creature walking upright near the Weber-Davis Canal. She didn't know what to make of the creature, which swung its arms back and forth as it walked, reported the *Standard-Examiner* in its edition of February 12, 1980. She saw it only briefly.

Another resident allegedly saw the same creature the next day, this time on his property in the dead of night. A winter moon bathed the sky as Ronald Smith went to feed his horses around midnight. He had just gotten home from work and the chore still needed to be done. As he went to the stables, he noticed something move out of the corner of his eye. He turned and, by the pale light of the moon, saw a dark figure walk across his property. He at first thought it was a teenager dressed in a hood, but then he heard what he described as "unearthly screams" and went back into his house. He didn't investigate until the next morning, when he found large footprints in the vicinity of where he saw the figure.

These were the only two people reported by the newspaper to have seen the creature, but others over the next few days claimed to have seen evidence of its visit to their own properties, including hearing strange noises, sensing obnoxious odors, and finding large footprints. In one case, more than one set of footprints was found at a particular residence. One set measured fifteen inches long, with a smaller set alongside it "as if the two beasts were walking hand in hand," the newspaper reported. On one property, strange hair was found in a barbed-wire fence. The hair was turned over to the state for analysis and could not at first be identified; it later was reported to be cow hair. Others reported that they had food stolen from their porches and that a rotten "stink" permeated near certain homes at odd hours of the day or night.

The article concluded that whatever it was that had made the ruckus apparently didn't like what it found in South Weber, because it vanished shortly after the reported incidences and hasn't been seen in the area since that strange week in February 1980. Monte Whaley, in an April 6, 1996, follow-up article in *The Salt Lake Tribune* wrote, "The tales hit the news, and Bigfoot hunters arrived en masse to chase down evidence. Even the state Division of Wildlife Resources launched a search for a Bigfoot, but found nothing to indicate it existed. Wildlife officials have declined to investigate further."

The Farmington Phantom

Unlike Washington Irving, whose name has been immortalized with the story of the Headless Horseman in "The Legend of Sleepy Hollow," John Burrows is little known to the reading public. Even many Farmington residents are unfamiliar with the local man's tales of a phantom—some say a headless phantom—that haunts the area near present-day Lagoon.

The story about the Farmington Phantom is likely nothing more than lore, according to an article in the *Standard-Examiner*, but that doesn't mean there aren't at least a few people who believe the story has merit.

The Farmington Phantom, as the story goes, is a dark-dressed spirit that rides atop a galloping ghost horse. Not many people in the ghostly presence actually see the shade; they are more likely to hear it. Those who have been privileged to see it, however, described it not unlike Irving's fictional Hessian. They claim it has no head or, at least, no face. According to the newspaper article, the first recorded sighting was made by Samuel Morgan in 1881, with other sightings reported in 1908 and 1935, always on the Old Canyon Road.

One witness, a man whose car became stranded while traveling through Farmington, heard the galloping horse and its dark rider. The stranded traveler was looking under the hood of his car when all of a sudden he heard a horse's hooves approach at high speed. The noise so startled him that he banged his head on the hood of his car, but when he looked to see what the ruckus was, there was no horse, no rider. Just the fast-clop sounds carried on the breeze.

If the story of the Farmington Phantom has any truth to it at all, what could it mean? We are left to wonder who the ghostly rider is and what his purpose is for riding shotgun on a dark steed at night in the middle of upper Utah.

Ghost Car at Viewmont High

When seventeen-year-old Debra Kent invited her parents to a school play, she thought it would be a pleasant evening to spend with her family. It started out that way, but because of a homicidal maniac, it ended in tragedy.

Before the family arrived at the school, they dropped off Kent's younger brother, not much inclined to school plays, at a nearby roller rink. Later in the evening, because the play was going longer than expected, Kent, a dark-haired beauty enjoying her last year of high school, offered to leave the play to pick her brother up at the rink so he wouldn't be stranded waiting for a ride. Her parents agreed to her proposal and gave her the keys to their car. She left the school's auditorium and was never seen again.

It later was learned that Kent, a student at Viewmont High School in Bountiful, became one of the victims of serial killer Ted Bundy's bloody rampage in the 1970s. It is believed that after Kent left the auditorium, she was asked by a man who greeted her in the parking lot to help him identify a car. When police investigated the parking lot later, they found a key belonging to a pair of handcuffs, believed to have been used on Kent by her abductor.

As for Bundy, perhaps the country's most notorious serial killer, he was first apprehended when he fled from police during a traffic stop in Granger, Utah. When police caught up with him, they found disturbing items in his car: handcuffs, an ice pick, and pantyhose with eye holes cut out. He was arrested for suspicion of burglary, and only later did evidence mount that he was the perpetrator behind a number of unsolved kidnappings and murders. Bundy, described as a "sadistic sociopath," reportedly confessed to murdering forty women—though it is believed he killed more than one hundred—in a dozen states between the years 1974 and 1978. After he was caught, he allegedly told police that Kent was among his victims. He gave authorities clues as to where he discarded Kent's remains, but all they found was a kneecap that was determined to have belonged to a young woman.

Bundy, who had escaped prison twice, was executed by electric chair on January 24, 1989, in Florida. Twenty-one years later, in February 2010, the serial killer's infamous 1968 Volkswagen Beetle was put on display at the National Museum of Crime and Punishment in Washington, D.C. At the unveiling stood "an unprepossessing tan Beetle, with a sunroof, looking a little worse for wear with touches of rust, fading paint and a few missing pieces of metal trim," wrote Philip Kennicott in a February 19, 2010, article for the *Washington Post*. "The tires looked as if they still had a few thousand good miles in them. Inside the cab, the interior had that quintessential old Bug smell—like burning latex—as if the rubber flooring was always smoking a little from the heat underneath. But this wasn't any Beetle. This was Ted Bundy's Beetle, the car into which he lured his victims and in which he killed many of them during a terrifying serial killing spree in the 1970s."

Another article on February 22, this one by Les Blumenthal for McClatchy Newspapers, read, "A 1976 Utah vehicle inspection sticker by the Utah State Patrol is still attached to the windshield. The front passenger seat is missing. Bundy removed it to make room for the bodies of his victims."

Though its physical form sits in the crime museum, legend has it that apparitions of the Beetle have been seen at the school where

Kent was abducted. Is this an urban legend made up about Kent's last known whereabouts? Or is there some truth to the story? Could it be that because there was so much evil and senseless tragedy associated with the Volkswagen that an apparition of it serves as a residual imprint at the scene of the crime?

The Ghosts of Union Station

Family members line up, waiting for the arrival of a train; their faces are flushed, their eyes wet with tears. The wait seems like forever, but before they know it, the clacking of wheels on tracks is heard, growing louder as the engines approach. A whistle sounds, but to the waiting family members it resembles a moan. And then the engines stop, but the tears keep coming. For some, they are a river. The family members wait not to welcome a visiting relative, but to retrieve the body of their deceased—most likely a father or husband or son. The waiting loved ones see people walk off the train, but the one whom they've come to greet is in a casket. The tears come faster now and the grieving family curses Adolf Hitler and the demigods of war. Just another day at the Grand Union Station in 1940s Ogden.

Trains were a big deal to Utah during the war and had been since the 1870s, when rail lines brought prospectors and businessmen to Ogden. Eventually, the city had nine rail systems that stretched in all directions. Area businesses flourished because of the trains, and Ogden for a time threatened to overshadow Salt Lake City in commerce. The railways brought success to area businesses, but they eventually also brought the bodies of dead servicemen home to their waiting, grieving families. During the war, it is estimated that 119 trains passed through Ogden for every twenty-four hour period. Some bodies of World War II servicemen were sent home to Utah without family members waiting for them at the station. These families would arrive later, but until they did, the bodies of the deceased had to be stored somewhere, so they were sent to the basement.

"It served as a kind of temporary morgue," said Kevin Erickson, director and founder of the Cache Paranormal Research Group. "There was a lot of sadness in there, where families would come to pick up their deceased." The railroad business declined after the war because of increasing competition from the automobile and airplane. By the 1950s, writes Richard Roberts in the *Encyclopedia of Utah*, passenger rail service was all but eliminated. But an aura of the war period remains. If you're in the right frame of mind you can sense today the melancholy that seems to be imprinted in the brick walls of the train station that now is a museum and restaurant. Erickson said at least one of the ghosts who haunt the building is an irritated card player. A room on the upper level once was used for gambling and carousing. While in the room one night, Erickson asked aloud if any of the spirits believed to still be there had ever cheated or been cheated while playing cards. EMF readings went off the charts, he said.

One woman, who wished to remain anonymous, said she felt uneasy when visiting the building in July 2009. She went with family to see the car, train, and gun museums inside the building. At the time she did not know of the building's melancholy history, but when walking its halls she felt kind of creepy. "I just felt that something went on there. I didn't know what it was," she said. "It wasn't an overwhelming feeling, but like there had been a presence there." Dark-shaded apparitions have been seen in the hallways, and objects, including a coat rack, have been seen moving on their own.

Even if it weren't for the very real ghosts that allegedly make the site their eternal roaming spot, the building would still be haunted— by the memory of the many dead soldiers who returned from the world's greatest conflict. In a very real sense, the building serves as kind of a testament to the ultimate sacrifice, Erickson said.

One of Utah's Most Haunted Buildings

In a quiet, unassuming spot in north Ogden sits the Union Stockyard Exchange building. The brown-brick facility that has Masonic symbols and the faces of farm animals etched into its façade sits behind a neatly trimmed lawn and a chain-link fence that keeps out trespassers. Its numerous windows stretch across the width of the building, and at first glance, the passerby might think it is an old schoolhouse. It has that look. And, depending on the day, if you peer at the windows closely enough, you might see a face staring back at you. It won't be a student, because after all, this is not a schoolhouse. But the face could be that of a young child, a cowboy, or one of three homicide victims killed in the building by an irate cattleman.

The triple homicide occurred on May 5, 1941, when an angry customer named Rodney Belnap entered the building, pulled out a gun, and fatally wounded Director Warren Felstedt and his two assistants, Joseph Boyer and Carolyn Johnson.

"This room is where the murders took place," investigator Kevin Erickson said about a third-story room on the far east end of the building. He was taking me on a tour of the building on a sunny, spring morning in early May 2011. The owners, Troy and LeAnna Reardon, had given Erickson unlimited access to the building because of its reputation as a haunted hot spot. In an ongoing paranormal investigation of the building, Erickson and his group have walked away with audio recordings, personal experiences, and a few unanswered questions such as "Why do the spirits of children haunt the facility?" It was never used as a place for children.

Troy was riding a lawnmower outside, which Erickson and I could hear as we walked the dark hallways inside. "Here is where the first suicide happened," he said about another room. And in yet another, "In here we caught audio of a boy drowning."

The building has seen its share of tragedy, something it was never intended to witness. The building was constructed in the 1930s as the offices of the Union Stockyard Exchange until 1968, when Weber County acquired the building and used it for a time as a place to treat mental health patients. Erickson said shock therapy and water therapy were used at the time. While it served as a mental health facility, three suicides allegedly occurred in the building. One woman, having cut herself on glass while jumping out a second-story window, bled to death on the lawn; a man hanged himself in an observation room; and another man jumped off the balcony, hitting his head on the tile floor below.

The Reardons acquired the building in 2004, when Troy purchased it for his wife as a Christmas present. Thereafter, the couple used it for a time as a Halloween attraction. During my visit to the building, decrepit costumes, half-mauled bodies, colorful blank-faced masks, and other Halloween props greeted us in many of the second-story rooms. In every way, it looked and felt like a haunted building. Red and rusty-colored stains were splashed on some of the walls. I had to ask, "That's fake blood, isn't it?" Erickson confirmed that it was.

But I couldn't help but to think about the real blood that had been spilt here. And the phantom noises, the free-moving doors, and the apparitions that have been seen in the building.

"That's where the girl was seen," Erickson said, pointing to a spot inside another room on the west end of the building's main floor. "She's been seen in broad daylight. What we've got from EVPs is that her name is Rebecca. When she's seen she seems to be around the nine to eleven mark, about yeah high, about three and a half to four foot with reddish brown hair, and wearing a white dress and is as solid as can be. When the owner first saw her, she thought she was a lost kid in the building. She walked right up to her and said 'Are you lost?' and she disappeared right in front of her."

Erickson doesn't know why the girl, and other children, are sometimes seen or heard in the building. He better understands why he saw a cowboy figure in the doorway of a room that used to be the facility's kitchen. "I walked down here (in April 2011) and froze like this, and he was right there," he said. The solid cowboy figure, which loomed about seven feet tall, had his hands in his pockets and was wearing a large-brimmed cowboy hat. "He was big, big . . . it scared the crap out of me," Erickson said, noting that he locked eyes with the figure for a good two or three seconds before the apparition faded away. "And then I could see all the details in the room again."

LeAnna said she's seen at least four spirits in the building—Rebecca, a little boy, and two men—at night and during the day. "Before this building I didn't believe in ghosts," LeAnna, who has a hearing disability, texted to me on June 10, 2011, "but after seeing a few I started to question both if they are real and my sanity." Her belief is not necessarily that ghosts are the result of traumatic events. If that were the case, "every inch of the earth would be haunted." She instead believes they are "other [dimension] visions. . . . Isaac Newton proved, mathematically, there are 27 [dimensions] and the veil between them is thin. They are our ghosts, we are theirs."

But how do you explain the next episode? On a Saturday in early February 2011, Erickson's group was investigating the building and was in the room with one of his team members where the homicide allegedly occurred. The team member, a woman, suddenly felt a sharp pain in her neck and soon was overcome with melancholy and pain. She started to cry and found it difficult to breathe. Erickson took her outside where she soon recovered. The woman, who did not know how the homicides had occurred inside the building, later found out that Carol, the female victim, had been shot in the neck. Did this investigator feel the phantom pain from a gunshot wound?

Though the Reardons have experienced odd, sometimes scary occurrences in the facility, they'd like to turn the building into something useful for the community, but LeAnna said so far the city has shot down all their ideas.

Interestingly, in a later phone interview in July 2011, Erickson said the atmosphere of the building had for some reason changed. "It's not a pleasant shift," he said, noting that his group was investigating the building about three weekends a month. "Something's going on; we don't know what it is. It's heavier, thicker. It feels draining."

Kay's Cross

For years a strange, enigmatic emblem attracted the curious to a remote hollow in Kaysville in Davis County. Getting to it wasn't easy, depending on the route you took. The difficult way was hiking up a hill and through Kaysville Cemetery, where local lore said would-be visitors to the hollow would confront malevolent guardian spirits.

Once in the hollow, if they made it past the ghostly guards, visitors would find a twenty-foot-high, thirteen-foot-wide stone cross. What's interesting about the cross was, well, just about everything. It was not exactly known by whom the cross was constructed or for what purpose. The mystery surrounding the cross lent itself to tall tales and urban legends, and the aforementioned one about the ghostly guardians is only one. Other stories told of devil worshippers who'd come to the hollow to perform sacrifices at the cross's base on Halloween nights, or that the face of a murder victim, allegedly a local wife, would appear in the cross on the anniversary of her death.

It is widely believed today that the cross, which no longer exists, was built by Eldon Kingston, an area landowner and polygamist, whose clan has a story stranger than fiction. In the 1920s, Kingston was associated with the prominent fundamentalists in Short Creek, Arizona. Mormon fundamentalists are not associated with the Church of Jesus Christ of Latter-day Saints, but are splinter groups that refuse to give up polygamy. By 1935, after the death of J. Leslie Broadbent, the group's leader, the Kingstons split from the Short Creek group and embraced the leadership of Eldon Kingston, Charles Kingston's son, believing he was the rightful successor. The Kingstons moved to Kaysville, where Eldon later claimed an angel had visited him, telling him to establish a communal society called the Davis County Cooperative Society.

Polygamy itself is a strange order, but perhaps even stranger is the story that says a body was encased inside the stone cross. The story proved a fable later, for the strange emblem was destroyed one night when for unknown reasons someone stuck dynamite inside it and blew it apart. No body was found to have been hidden inside the cross.

Even if these weird stories about the cross are not true, its very existence was strange enough. Since urban legends often have truth to them, what's the truth behind the ghostly stories about the cross and the quiet hollow?

The Boy Spirit of Steed's Pond

A popular ghost story in Clearfield, a suburb in Davis County, is about the spirit of a young boy who haunts Holt Elementary School and the nearby pond where he drowned. According to the story, which has become something of lore over the years, the male student, sometime in the 1980s, walked to Steed's Pond to go swimming one day after school. He went into the pond but never came back out. It's rumored that teachers and students over the years have often seen the boy's spirit, dressed in soggy T-shirt and shorts, near the back steps of the school, the door from which he supposedly left on his fateful journey to the pond. The ghost doesn't stick around for long, though, but in its place it leaves behind wet puddles and footprints.

People who visit the pond where the boy drowned have reported hearing phantom cries and calls for help. Some believe this story is nothing more than local lore, because others who come to the pond to fish have reported nothing more than catching a few rainbow trout. The pond today is owned by the city of Clearfield and sits on the twenty-three-acre Charles E. Steed Memorial Park next to the elementary school. Besides fishing, the park has four tennis courts, three softball fields, two volleyball courts, a walking path, playground, concessions, and a picnic shelter. The park is named after the original owner of the property.

Clearfield is big on family fishing, and Steed's Pond is the thirty-eighth fishing pond in the city. The pond has been fished in for years, but improved in 2009 when the city council passed a resolution that put the Utah Division of Wildlife Resources in charge of managing the pond's fish population.

If you come here to catch your limit of hatchery-stocked rainbows, just be sure to keep your ears attuned to the netherworlds. You just might hear those ghostly calls for help.

Salt Lake Valley

IF UTAH HAS A HEART, IT IS SALT LAKE CITY. IT IS A CLEAN, WELL-organized city with many historic buildings and architectural marvels. While it is the state's hub, it is but one city in a valley that has many. The valley itself is bordered east and west by two scenic mountain ranges and capped at the far northwest by the Great Salt Lake, for which the city and valley is named. Here among the beauty and hustle and bustle of daily life are several haunted hot spots. Read on and learn about a historic park where the pioneer spirit, in more ways than one, is alive and well; a stately theater that's inhabited by a friendly spirit named George; the ghostly legend of an 1800s grave robber; haunted houses; and more.

Haunted Heritage

If you like history, you'll love This Is the Place Heritage Park in Salt Lake City. As you tour the site, the past comes alive perhaps like no other place in the state. The park, operated by This Is the Place Heritage Foundation, memorializes a period in Utah and the West that no longer exists except in places like the park.

Brigham Young, an enigmatic character who led Latter-day Saints on their westward journey in 1847, caught his first glimpse of the Salt Lake Valley at what now is called Emigration Canyon.

31

Looking over the fertile valley on a warm July 24, Young said, "It is enough. This is the right place." The Mormons, who had fled persecution in the Midwest, had found their home. Just three years before, on June 27, 1844, Mormon founder Joseph Smith was killed by a mob in Carthage, Illinois. Anti-Mormons thought the death of Smith would put an end to the Mormon movement. They were wrong. If anything, his death fueled it further. Young, the leading member of the church's Quorum of Twelve Apostles, succeeded Smith as church president, though it wasn't until after the great migration that he officially was appointed to that position.

On the very day that Young gazed across the valley, another fifteen thousand Mormons started on the trail from Ohio. Over the next two years, more than sixty thousand Latter-day Saints would make the migration westward. Once they entered the Salt Lake Valley, the Latter-day Saints spread out, establishing communities across the Wasatch Front and beyond. The neatly organized streets and communities are testaments to the determination of the Mormon pioneers and those of other faiths, who after 1847 eked out a living in the arid climate of one of the country's most beautiful and promising states. This Is the Place Heritage Park, as its name suggests, helps preserve that heritage. In more ways than one, it preserves the pioneer spirit.

Ask a staff member or two and they could probably tell you stories about some of the strange happenings that go on at the park. There is nothing evil here. But they tell stories of things that can't be explained except in the context of the paranormal. More than fifty historic buildings sit on the 450-acre parcel. Many of these buildings allegedly have resident ghosts.

Balls of self-illuminating light have been seen floating in the upstairs rooms of the 1860s-era Brigham Young Farmhouse, said historical interpreter Kendra Babitz. She witnessed the lights one night while waiting for visitors in October 2008. Though the balls of light were seen during a Halloween attraction, she said there is no logical explanation for what she witnessed. She was the only person in the house at the time, and the lights grew and dimmed as they floated on the second story.

Babitz said she believes the entities in the farmhouse could be the spirits of children. It is believed that Brigham Young never lived

in the farmhouse himself, but his many wives did. Young is reported to have had fifty-seven wives. Each took turns living in the house. "They never lived there together," Babitz said. Young did use the house, which originally was located in present-day Sugarhouse, as a showplace to host dignitaries. The upstairs was used as a play area, where the children often hung out. The house was moved to the park in the mid-1970s, and over the years there have been a number of strange occurrences reported in the house, and the self-illuminating balls of light story is only one.

In the Hiram L. Andrus home, a spirit, presumably of a woman, likes things quiet after 9:30 at night. On more than one occasion during special events at the park, staff would plug the cords of small stereos into the walls to play music inside the house. Then, when they least expected it, the music would suddenly stop. When staff would go to check on the problem, they'd find the stereo unplugged, the cord lying two feet away from the wall. No one else was inside the house to play the prank, Babitz said. They'd plug the cord back into the wall and the stereo would play. They'd leave the room and the music would stop. When they returned they'd find the cords again unplugged.

Like the Young house, Babitz said she's never felt anything malevolent at the Andrus home, though she sometimes has felt unwelcome, as if the resident ghost was saying, "This is my house and you don't belong here," especially after 9:30 at night. Maybe that is the ghost's bedtime, or the time in life when she put the children to bed.

"Diamond" Jim Davis, another historical interpreter, said he's experienced a number of unexplained phenomena since he started working at the park. Some of his experiences include hearing phantom footsteps and seeing an apparition. He recounts his experiences saying, "I never used to believe in the paranormal until I started working at Heritage Park."

His witness of an apparition happened one snowy February morning. While driving up the hill toward the Mary Fielding Smith house, he saw a Mormon Battalion soldier dressed in period clothing. He at first thought the figure was an actor, because a film crew had recently been filming on park grounds, but as he came closer to the house the image slowly faded.

Mary was the wife of church patriarch Hyrum Smith, who had been killed with his brother Joseph in Carthage, Illinois. She was a devout and strict woman. Because the Latter-day Saints had been driven by mobs from their former homes, Davis said, Mary seemed to take great pride in the home she established in the Salt Lake Valley. Her home was first located at 2700 South 1300 East and moved to the park in 1979 or 1980. Davis said he believes the spirit he saw that wintry morning was a former member of the Mormon Battalion sent to guard Mary's house.

Davis shares another memorable experience, this one occurring one day while working in the park's saddle shop, the B. F. Johnson Saddlery. As often is the case, he was working alone, trying to put together a leather knife sheath. But it wasn't going well, he said. The glue wasn't holding. After a few minutes of trying to get the glue to hold, he left the building frustrated, returning about twenty minutes later. To his surprise, he found the sheath lying on a chair, glued together. His first thought was that someone else at the park completed it for him, but only two other people were on the grounds that morning—a desk worker and a visitor, both in other buildings. Besides, he said, how could another person make the glue stick when he couldn't?

If you haven't been to the park, you've missed something. And as paranormally active as the park might be, weird things don't occur every day, Babitz said. And they don't usually occur if you're expecting them to. When they do happen, it's when staff least expect them, often while they go about their responsibilities, their minds focused elsewhere.

Babitz and Davis both said they've never felt threatened at the park—and the stories they've heard from other staff members say the same—but they can't explain the weird things they've experienced. Asked if he believes if there are any conflicts with Mormon theology and his experiences with the paranormal, Davis said no. Mormons believe God has a plan for human beings, including their spirits once they die. They believe the spirit world is on the earth, same as mortals, only in another sphere. "It makes sense that if they're here," Davis said, "perhaps we can catch glimpses of them from time to time."

Violent Phantoms?

Josh Bryant, an investigator with the Cache Paranormal Research Society, led an investigative team inside the City and County Building, one of Salt Lake's oldest structures. During the investigation, the group recorded shadow play in the basement—a phantom figure moving in and out of camera vision. All else, for the most part, was quiet. When the group closed down for the night, Bryant went upstairs to make sure the doors were locked and the lights were turned off. While on the fifth floor he felt a tug on his shirt, as if his clothing had got caught on a nail. He didn't think much about it until he got down to the third floor. His shoulder and back were beginning to burn. Maybe it wasn't a nail after all, he thought. Maybe a bug bit him. By the time he got to the first level, his back was burning so badly that he asked his teammates to take a look. He lifted his shirt, and they were shocked by what they saw: three red fingernail scratches running down his back.

"I've been touched before," Bryant said about his ghostly encounters, "but never scratched. This was a first for me." For days afterward, Bryant was disturbed by what had happened to him. If he began to doubt the experience, the scratch marks quickly reminded him of the reality of it.

The Gothic-looking structure that is the City and County Building sits on a ten-acre parcel called Washington Square in downtown Salt Lake City. Constructed in 1894 and adorned by a clock tower whereon stands the statue Columbia, it was intended to rival the LDS church's Salt Lake Temple as the city's architectural centerpiece. Building a facility that both city and county government could use was a major issue in 1880s Utah. In an executive session on December 18, 1888, presided over by Mayor Francis Armstrong, members of the Salt Lake County Court proposed to join with the city in building a city hall-courthouse. The city concurred, but neither entity could agree on a location to build the facility. It was planned first at First South and First East, but later was changed to its current location at Washington Square, at the time named the Eighth Ward Square. The site had served the pioneers ever since they arrived in the valley. Pioneers on their way to California and Oregon also would stop here to rest and refresh their supplies, often greeted by welcoming parties who'd offer them food and drinks.

Later, the site was used to host carnivals and other celebrations, and even baptisms. As early as 1859, however, Washington Square was considered to be the property of Salt Lake City.

Today, Washington Square, with its expansive lawn, statues, and numerous shade trees, has all the makings of a park. City festivities and civic gatherings often are held here beneath the shadow of the Gothic-looking structure. But it's inside the building where the ghosts hang out. Bryant isn't the only one to claim interaction with a ghost inside the building. It's one of the city's most popular allegedly haunted sites, often discussed in paranormal circles and on websites dealing with folklore and urban legends. Apparitions of children have been reported on the fourth floor, and visitors and staff have heard footsteps, laughter, and doors slam. Lights have been known to turn off and on by themselves, and there have been reports of temperature fluctuations. More than one person has claimed to have been touched or grabbed by unseen hands while in the building.

The Enigma of Lilly E. Gray

Utah's most famous cemetery, where the bodies of prophets and paupers are buried, rests atop a tree-filled hillside in Salt Lake City's Avenues District. The 250-acre Salt Lake City Cemetery has a lush lawn, which, besides the trees, is dotted with crosses, statues, mausoleums, and a variety of headstones both flat and tall. The cemetery has more than nine miles of road and is considered the largest city-operated cemetery in the United States; it is estimated to be the eternal resting place for the bodies of more than 120,000 people, both the state's famous and infamous. Prominent businessmen, politicians, and religious leaders lie beneath its soil or are encased in its crematorium.

Grave markers, in a sense, attest to the classes and religions of the dearly departed. Some of the headstones here are elaborately adorned; others are simple creations with names and dates. Some of the grave markers have curious inscriptions, but perhaps none as curious as the headstone belonging to Lilly E. Gray. Those who come upon it usually walk away feeling a bit disturbed by the inscription:

LILLY E. GRAY
JUNE 6, 1881-NOV 14, 1958
VICTIM OF THE BEAST 666

The headstone's inscription has haunted graveyard visitors for years. While some might take a fleeting look, fighting off the shivers that roil on their skin after reading the devilish inscription, others have spent a lot of time trying to unmask the mystery that surrounds Lilly Gray, or, as her obituary has her name, Lily Gray. Gray's obituary lists her first name and birth date differently than what is engraved on the headstone. And it misspells the name Elko, Nevada: "Mrs. Lily Edith Gray, 78, 1216 Pacific Ave., died Friday, 11:10 a.m., in a Salt Lake hospital of natural causes. Born June 4, 1880, Canada. Salt Lake resident since 1950. Married Elmer Lewis Gray, July 10, 1952, Elco, NV. Survivors: Husband; several nieces and nephews."

The alleged truth behind the enigma, however, is that her husband, Elmer, was a cantankerous man who held obvious contempt for the law. On March 15, 1947, Elmer filed an application for a term of pardons or parole. He was arrested, though it's unclear for what. After writing his name, Elmer crossed out the word "serving" and replaced it with the word "kidnaped," referring to his arrest by police officers. In another place that asks where his parents live, he wrote, "Booth Dead. Died of grief when kidnapers murdered my [first] Wife." His responses to the questions on the parole sheet show his apparent contempt for government and the law, whom he blamed for his wife's death. But why he'd want to mark his second wife's grave with such a devilish inscription, one that would last into the undetermined future, is haunting in its own right.

Emo's Grave

One of the more popular urban legends about the Salt Lake Cemetery concerns the gravesite of Jacob Moritz, more popularly known as "Emo," though it is unclear how he was given that name. The story of Emo has circulated for decades. It goes something like this.

Emo, depending on which version of the story you hear, was either a child molester or devil worshipper who was burned alive for his crimes. The vigilantes placed his ashes in an urn and sealed it inside a mausoleum in the Salt Lake Cemetery. The restless spirit of Emo allegedly has haunted his gravesite ever since, for he will appear to anyone who circles his tomb and chants the name "Emo" three times.

Teenage boys perhaps have had the most fun with this story, taking young women to the graveyard in hopes that their frightened dates would jump into their arms. As with most urban legends, the story of Emo has been passed on for so long that it's difficult to tell how or when the story started. The real story of Emo Moritz isn't nearly as scary as the legend.

Simply, Moritz was a Jewish business owner. It could be that the story of Emo started long ago by sensationalists in Mormon-heavy Salt Lake Valley as a slight against the Jewish brewer.

If you'd like to visit Emo's grave, perhaps to see if there's something to the legend after all, it is located in the southern part of the cemetery, just east of P Street. If you have trouble finding it, get a map of the cemetery that will point you to the gravesites of the ground's most famous and infamous. Just be sure when you find Moritz's marker that you circle it and chant three times the name "Emo."

Earthbound Angels: The Three Nephites

It's interesting to me that some people who claim they don't believe in the supernatural or paranormal have fond affections for sacred literature that often is filled with stories of the supernatural. The Bible, for instance, talks about angels, spirits, witches, and demons. The Bible, which literally means "book of books," also tells of miraculous healings, dead people being brought back to life, and of John the Revelator, also known as "John the beloved" or "the disciple whom Jesus loved," tarrying upon the Earth until the Second Coming of Jesus Christ. At least, that's the way the Mormons view the following passage from the Book of John, in which the Apostle Peter inquires of Jesus what it is he wished the disciple to do. "Feed my sheep," Jesus replied three times. After this, continues John, "Peter seeing him [John] saith to Jesus, 'Lord, and what shall this man do?' Jesus saith unto him, 'If I will that he tarry till I come, what is that to thee?' . . . Then went this saying abroad among the brethren, that that disciple should not die." (See John 21:15-23.)

According to Mormon belief, before Jesus left his disciples, he caused a change called "translation" to come upon John. Translation, according to the theology, is a state in between mortality and immortality, wherein the subject is neither mortal nor immortal but is able to withstand the vicissitudes of the mortal experience. John, it is believed, remains on the Earth and will do so until Jesus returns. Mormons also believe that at least three other ancients, like John, remain upon the earth. These men, who lived in America during the time of Christ, are popularly called the Three Nephites (pronounced "Knee-fites"), referred to in the Book of Mormon.

Ever since the church was organized in 1830 in Upstate New York, stories about these earth-bound angels have circulated in Mormondom, especially once the pioneers arrived in the Salt Lake Valley. Occasionally a new story about the Three Nephites pops up in Mormon circles, especially in the mission fields, but most of the known stories are those that rose during the pioneer days. These divinely selected men allegedly would show up at the homes of faithful Latter-day Saints to minister a blessing: A farmer, burdened with planting his crop, wakes one morning to find that his fields have been prepped and plowed during the night; a housewife who, after a knock at her door, feeds a stranger only to find that ever after her family's cupboards are miraculously filled with food. Such is one story that Michael Norman and Beth Scott share in their book, *Haunted America*.

Salt Lake City, 1852: A man knocks on a door. A woman answers. The man, dressed rather shabbily, tells her that he's in need of a meal. Could she help him? The woman, knowing her own family is struggling economically, hesitates only a moment before inviting the stranger inside. She directs the man to the kitchen table and then goes about preparing him a plate of food. It wasn't much by today's standards, but it was all the woman could afford to give the stranger: bread, onions, and a glass of water.

The man eats quickly, tackling the food as if he hadn't eaten in days. When he finishes, he thanks the woman for her hospitality and asks what he owes her. The woman declines money, saying that she was happy to be of help. The man, a smile breaking on his face, says: "May God bless you. Peace be with you!"

Later, as hardship, distress, and drought afflicted this family's neighbors, the matriarch of the house somehow always found her larder filled enough to provide meals for her family. Having never gone hungry since the stranger's visit, the woman believed the blessing had something to do with the man who one day unexpectedly showed up at her door.

This story has the feel of a religious allegory, similar to Jesus's parable of feeding the stranger (see Matthew 25:34-40), but such stories were commonplace in 1800s Utah. Are any of the stories, contemporary or otherwise, about the Three Nephites real or are they all made up to correlate with the faith's own Book of Mormon? The book not only discusses the Three Nephites' "translation" but their later ministry, including a visit they made to Mormon, the book's primary author and historian who lived about four hundred years after Jesus blessed the Three Nephites. "I have seen them," Mormon writes, "and they have ministered unto me."

Like most supernatural events, deemed religious or otherwise, it is difficult if not impossible to confirm. And while very few Latter-day Saints claim they've experienced encounters with John the Revelator or the Three Nephites, a great many Mormons believe that these ancient men really do remain alive upon the Earth today. Just in case that's true, you might want to offer an extra "thank you" if in a time of need you're ever approached by a stranger willing to help; or agree to provide a meal if someone comes knocking on your door asking for a bite to eat.

Noises in the Attic

There's a house in southern Salt Lake County that is visited every evening by a dancing ghost. Well, maybe not a "dancing" ghost, but it likes to make a ruckus when it walks across the attic floor, which it does every evening between the hours of five and six, the sound of its footsteps echoing throughout the multi-level house.

The home's occupant said she isn't frightened by the noisy visitor. Though she laughed when she talked about her unseen house guest, noting that the noise probably is just the house settling, she doesn't understand other strange phenomena that have happened at the home. The orbs, for instance.

A number of orbs have been caught on film at the house, but nothing quite as unnerving as one day after a funeral when a cluster of them appeared in a digital photo. A sequence of shots had been taken at the same angle in the same room, one right after another. No orbs in photo one. No orbs in photo two or three; the same for photo four. But in photo five there appeared a cluster of orbs, grouped together as if forming a face. The skeptical family members paid the pictures little attention, believing the orbs to be dust or another anomaly. Those inclined to believe in the weird wondered if the orbs were the energy influence of their dead relative.

Orbs are not new phenomena—they've shown up on film for years. The proliferation of digital technology, however, has increased the "orb awareness." The technology has, in fact, allowed investigators to better study orbs, which some believe are nothing more than dust, moisture, lens flares, reflections, or slow shutter speeds. "Still," explains paranormal writer Rosemary Ellen Guiley in her online article "Reevaluating Orbs," "even the hardest skeptics acknowledge that at least a tiny percentage of orb photos cannot be explained. Perhaps it is true what orb enthusiasts say: that our improved photographic technology is enabling us to capture evidence of life forms that are intelligent and are below the register of the human eye." One theory is that orbs are not spirits themselves but energy being transferred from a source to the spirit so it can manifest itself. Is that what happened in this instance? It is a question that as yet is left unanswered.

As for the attic noises, though the homeowner said they're likely caused by the house settling, they seem to happen all year long at the same time—in summer when the days are long, and in winter when the sun sets in late afternoon. Wouldn't the house settle at different times of the day, depending on the season? On the other hand, why would a ghost haunt her attic? There's nothing up there but insulation and a few boxes.

A haunted house—every town has one. You might know of someone who claims their house is haunted, or perhaps you've had your own experience with things that go bump in the night. The term "haunt" comes from the same root word as "home." Thus, places considered haunted often are the former homes of the deceased. A haunting doesn't always involve seeing an apparition. Often it's simply a noise, smell, or sensation. It is a common belief among paranormal groups that there are at least six different classifications:

- **Residual.** When a traumatic event occurs, the negative energy of the episode is, in a sense, imprinted on or recorded in the atmosphere and often repeats itself over and over again. Most of the hauntings in Utah, especially at historic places and houses, are believed to be residual in nature.
- **Intelligent.** Once in a while a wary homeowner or ghost-buster will encounter an intelligent haunting, which is interaction with a spirit that responds to questions or activity. The entity is aware of our presence and can touch or in other ways communicate with us. About ten percent of Utah house hauntings are considered to be intelligent.
- **Poltergeist.** Believed to be human-caused, poltergeists often are associated with adolescents, especially teenage girls going through hormonal changes that cause a lot of pent-up energy; poltergeists are believed to be projected by the mind, causing objects to move, making tapping sounds, turning on and off lights, and so on.
- **Demons.** The malicious spirits of unearthly beings that scare, torment, and often manipulate people to commit sinful acts are believed to be demons. They are evil entities that often appear as black fog, mist, shadow, or misleading spirits. Demon hauntings are rare. It is believed that it takes a religious force, such as blessing or exorcism, to resolve this type of haunting.
- **Shadow People.** Different from ghosts, shadow people are still an enigma. They usually are shapeless, dark masses, mostly seen with your peripheral vision. They can move between walls but have no human features. Clairvoyants consider them non-human entities. Shadow figures have been reported at historic places, restaurants, malls, and homes.
- **Doppelganger.** If you look out of the corner of your eye and you happen to see yourself, perhaps standing in a crowded room or walking by on the sidewalk, this is a doppelganger, considered to be the evil twin and the harbinger of misfortune or death. Doppelgangers are extremely rare.

"It's really tough being an investigator in Utah because we know that half of the houses here are haunted, but nobody wants to come forth and say, 'Yeah, they're haunted,'" said investigator Joshua

Bryant, noting that his own home in Murray has been the site of unwanted phantom guests.

"I saw a full-bodied figure up close," he said. "I woke up one night and felt this overwhelming feeling of dread and of fear like I never felt before. I was paralyzed with fear, like right when you're going to die, a finality of fear. This was in the basement. I could see its head and shoulders . . . looking at me right in the face. I'd never been more scared in my life. I closed my eyes for a minute and said, 'You need to go away. You need to go away.' . . . We don't know if it was a residual haunting or what it was. It was the only time I felt threatened, and I still get this creeped-out feeling when I think about it."

His home sits in Murray's historic district, not far from the city cemetery. Before it was a cemetery for the modern dead, it was a hallowed spot to the Orai Indians, who'd come and rest at the spot during the cold months. When spring came around, they'd bury those of their group who had died during winter. When the pioneers arrived and began burying their own dead at the same location, they disrespected the Indians by removing their bones and placing them in a mass grave nearby. "I'm almost one hundred-percent sure that this was an Orai Indian trying to tell me something: To treat this land with respect," Bryant said about his strange visitor. At other times in his house, Bryant has heard phantom footsteps in the basement.

Another place or two where a number of alleged hauntings occur is in Magna and West Valley, also known as the "Granite District." "To be honest," Bryant said, "any case that we've done in Magna, we've got some sort of activity." Most of it has been residual in nature, though once in a while his group will encounter an intelligent haunting. The reason why the area is paranormally active is because of its often violent past, including its mine disasters, and because the landscape is built upon a granite foundation. "There's a reason why it's called the Granite District," Bryant said, explaining that granite has been known to trap residual activity, allowing events to be played over and again.

If you've experienced strange occurrences in your home that make you doubt your previous assumptions about life after death, Bryant has a message: "Don't feel stigmatized because you're having things go on that you can't explain. . . . Religion and the paranormal can exist side by side; people just look at things the wrong way."

George, the Friendly Ghost

The Phantom of the Opera, a classic horror novel written by French journalist Gaston Leroux, tells a captivating story about love and loss. The book's antagonist, ghostly Erik, haunts the Paris Opera House and has season tickets, if you will, in his favorite seat of Box Five.

Likewise, a prankster ghost called George is believed by some to haunt the Capitol Theater, one of the state's most elegant buildings in downtown Salt Lake City. It is not known if this ghost, like Leroux's possessive phantom, has a favorite seat, but it does seem to get a kick out of interacting with the theater's staff.

George, who was named by retired security officer Doug Morgan, is believed to be the spirit of a young usher killed in a fire that occurred in the theater in 1947. Apparently, George has a sense of humor, for a number of theater workers, including Morgan, have said they've been the butt of the spirit's pranks. In an October 31, 2001, article in *The Salt Lake Tribune*, Morgan told reporter Tom Wharton that during the 1978 opening of *The Nutcracker*, George fooled with the lights. "We were down to five minutes to show time and I was exasperated," Morgan said. "How do you put on a *Nutcracker* without lights? I looked up and said, 'Damn it, George, knock it off or I am going to have you exorcised.' And the lights came back on."

Others who've experienced interaction with unseen entities in the building say the third floor is a hot spot for paranormal activity, as is the theater's projection booth. People claim to have been touched by unseen hands and felt cold spots and drastic temperature reductions. Some investigators say they've recorded ghost voices. In one instance a recording was determined to have said, "Touched" and "I hate you." These episodes likely are not caused by George, a friendly prankster, because they seem out of character for him; they are possibly from other entities that may inhabit the century-old theater.

The Capitol Theater, originally part of the Orpheum chain of theaters, was built in 1913 as a place to showcase vaudeville acts, which were popular for several decades in the late 1800s and early 1900s. Designed by Albert G. Lansburgh, who graduated from the Ecole des Beaux Arts in Paris, the building "incorporated classic design and was stylistically advanced for its time," reads a historical plaque about the building. "The theater's highly decorative Italian Renaissance–style is significant as an innovation in the development of Utah architecture." It included modern mechanical and safety features, including fireproof and earthquake-resistant construction and air conditioning.

Sixteen years after it opened, the building was acquired by Salt Lake City mayor Louis Marcus, who gave it a new name, expanded its seating capacity, and showed its first talking picture.

As with men, the years took its toll on the building. Resurrection Day came in 1976, when Salt Lake County purchased the building and restored it closely to its original form, becoming the city's grand performing arts center. People today visit the theater not to encounter a ghost but to see the professional productions performed here, such as *The Nutcracker*, one of the most popular. Andrew Lloyd Webber's popular rendition of *The Phantom of the Opera* also has been performed here, which perhaps is only fitting considering the theater's paranormal history. I wonder if George liked it.

The Old Mill

In a time when newspapers are experiencing the challenges of trying to adjust to the digital age, it seems almost old-fashioned to discuss paper mills. But paper has played an important role for much longer. Utah once had a number of paper mills, including one built by the *Deseret News* in 1883 at the mouth of Big Cottonwood Canyon in present-day Cottonwood Heights. During its heyday over the next nine years, the mill produced five tons of paper a day. Product to make paper came from logs retrieved from nearby canyons and rags from church members.

The Granite Paper Mills Company acquired the mill in 1892, and a year later, on April 1, 1893, a fire broke out inside the building. Fueled by the paper inside, the fire ravaged the structure until all that remained was a skeletal frame. It wasn't until 1927 that the building was partially rebuilt; it then was used for various functions over the ensuing decades, including as an open-air dance hall and a haunted house attraction. In 1966, the Daughters of the Utah Pioneers declared the mill a historic site. The city of Cottonwood Heights, however, declared it condemned in 2005.

And condemned it is, for over the years it has been rumored to be one of the valley's most haunted buildings. People who've visited said they've encountered cold spots, heard sounds of growling, and felt an oppressive spirit on the grounds. Self-illuminating lights also have been reported inside the building. Warning: The Old Mill is privately owned and there is no trespassing allowed.

The Legend of John Baptiste

The ghost of a former gravedigger is said to haunt the southern shores of the Great Salt Lake. This lonely spirit, who is rumored to be seen clutching his soggy clothes, aimlessly wanders the shores in search of anyone he can share a few moments with.

The story of John Baptiste (some reports say his name was "Jean") is one of the more popular tales in Utah. For our intents and purposes, the Frenchman's story begins on January 27, 1862, with the exhumation of the body of Moroni Clawson.

Clawson was one of eight men accused of robbing a stagecoach and assaulting its prime occupant, Utah governor John W. Dawson. The other perpetrators included Wood Reynolds, Lot Huntington, Ike Niebaur, Jason Luce, Mat Luce, and Wilford Luce.

Dawson wrote a letter to the editor of the *Deseret News*, published in the newspaper's January 22, 1862, edition. "Sir," the letter began, "I deem it an act of justice to make a plain statement of the circumstances connected with the brutal and unprovoked attack made on me at Mountain Dell, Ephraim Hanks' mail station, on the night of the 31st ultimo. . . . I suspected nothing wrong until I had got nearly out of town, when Ephraim Hanks rode up and said that there were some desperate men in the city who it was possible might follow me for violence or plunder, but he rather thought not. I then asked him to go with me to his station as his appearance there would insure immunity from assault, should any be intended; but he said it was impossible for him to go, but he would go back and send Moroni Clawson, who would do just as well as he would."

Hanks was wrong, for in the same letter Dawson called Clawson "the traitor" who acted as friend but set him up for the attack. It apparently wasn't the gang's first offense, for Dawson said the "desperadoes" had "cast another stain on the city, as they have heretofore often done." Dawson ended his letter by asking for a "speedy trial and condign punishment."

For some of the gang members, their trial ended with ball and pistol. Huntington, while trying to flee, was gunned down January 16, 1862, in Tooele by Mormon vigilante Porter Rockwell. Clawson and another man suffered the same fate a few days later when they were shot to death for trying to flee from police near Second South in Salt Lake City. All three were buried in the Salt Lake Cemetery. Until George Clawson showed up, that is, to claim the body of his dead brother. When the grave was exhumed on January 27, George was shocked to find the body of his brother lying face-down in the coffin and as naked as the day he was born. George was furious. Why had his brother been buried in such a manner? He demanded an investigation. Enter John Baptiste.

One day during surveillance of the cemetery, Baptiste, a gravedigger employed by the city, was caught pushing a wheelbarrow full of clothes, while a naked corpse was found lying in a nearby cemetery bush. George Clawson and "three or four other men" searched Baptiste's house while the gravedigger was away, though his wife was home, and soon found enough evidence to convict the gravedigger of grave robbing—boxes of dead men's clothes. Officials believed the clothing and jewelry had been stolen from at least 350 bodies he had interred. Families were hurt and angered at the ghoulish activity of Baptiste, who was described by one newspaper writer as "entirely conscienceless."

Should Baptiste be killed for his crimes? Brigham Young said no, that if it were left up to him, he would "make him a fugitive and vagabond upon the earth." The idea was hatched: Baptiste was to be banished to Fremont Island in the Great Salt Lake. This is where the story gets interesting.

After providing him with a shanty and provisions, the officers left him alone on the island. They returned about three weeks later to refresh the food supply and found Baptiste "was getting along very well in his loneliness." Satisfied, the officers left; but when they again returned to the island a few weeks later they didn't find any trace of their prisoner's whereabouts. They left the island puzzled. Did Baptiste somehow escape the island or did he take his own life? There's no official record of his body being found, though some believed a human skull found by a group of hunters at the mouth of the Jordan River, where it empties into the lake, belonged to the unscrupulous grave robber.

"There are only two tenable theories as to Baptiste's fate: either that he perished in the Lake in attempting to reach the mainland, or that he really succeeded," reads a June 3, 1893 article in the *Deseret News*. "That he died on the island is wholly disbelieved, because during the years that have elapsed since, every foot of it has been traversed at least a score, perhaps a hundred times, by sheepmen and cattlemen, and no trace of his remains has ever been found." The same article said that some people believed Baptiste made his way to Promontory and on to Montana, where later it was allegedly reported he was seen working the mines; others believed he joined an emigrant party and headed to San Francisco, and then to Southern California where he died.

It's likely that the fate of Baptiste will remain a mystery. As will the rumor about his spirit walking the southern shores of the ancient lake, his soggy clothes clutched in his arms. Some have claimed that they've heard his anguished cries in the dead of night, sorry for the misdeeds he committed in the flesh that led to his isolation. Perhaps his spirit, tired of being alone, is trying to get people's attention. Maybe he's trying to ask for forgiveness, a pardon for his misdeeds.

Haunted Magna

I sat alone in the small newsroom, a large picture window in front of me that looked out onto Main Street, and on my desktop a half-written story. It was a quiet morning, the kind I enjoyed in order to get things done.

The *Magna Times*, owned by Howard and Bonnie Stahle, had served the community since 1907. Its cozy, ink-filled building is just as old. The Stahles, who acquired the building in the early 1970s, worked long and hard to make it a vibrant voice in the community. They eventually opened two other weekly newspapers, one to serve nearby West Valley and the other to serve the township of

Kearns. I worked as the newspaper's managing editor for two years, from 2004 to 2006, overseeing the production of all three papers, and at a transitional time for the struggling business. I helped pull it into modernity—or, as its masthead reminded me every day, the "Times"—by initiating its own website and tackling broader-based stories than its previous writers had covered. It was an uphill battle, however, both economically and practically, and I eventually pursued greener pastures at larger newspapers.

I still have fond memories working for the *Magna Times*, now called the *Oquirrh Times*, and enjoyed sitting in its spacious, musty newsroom, where in front of my desk a large picture window looked out onto the town's historic Main Street. At the time, there wasn't much new about Magna. Everything seemed old—from the brown-brick buildings to the dust-covered newspapers that sat tucked inside cabinet walls to the alleged ghosts that still haunt the now more modern-looking Magna. Here is one experience I had while working at the newspaper.

One morning while working on a story, I heard the presses in the backroom begin to roll. That's interesting, I thought. Nothing should be printed today. I got up from my desk and walked to the pressroom, finding it empty and quiet. Was it just my imagination? I wondered.

And then a figure walked across the back of the room. "Carlos," I called. No answer.

I followed him into the dark room, which was located in back of the press and to the right. I entered the room and was greeted by darkness. I called again: "Carlos." Again, no answer.

I turned on the light. The room was empty. He couldn't have gone elsewhere, because there was only one door, and I was standing in its entryway.

Had I just witnessed a residual haunting in the historic building, or was it strictly my imagination? Whether it was paranormal or not, I figured there were ghosts here anyway—in the paper's archives where the stories of people past and present seemed just as fresh as the day they came off the presses. In that way their memories live on, their ghosts speak. But there are other stories.

In the summer of 2004, I wrote a newspaper article about the demise of the Webster School building, just a few blocks to the west of the newspaper. It had stood vacant for several years before it was destroyed by an arson fire. Its only occupants during the time it sat vacant were vagrants and, according to rumor, a few spirits.

After the fire, what remained of the building was later razed. I wrote the article for the *Magna Times*, and later earned a first-place award for the story in that year's statewide newspaper contest. While I reveled in my win, people who knew Webster better than I came to collect bricks from the old schoolhouse. It apparently held fond memories for the folks who once attended school there, and even the ghosts, while the building stood vacant, couldn't seem to leave Webster behind.

Ghost hunters and others who visited the building over the years claimed to have heard the bustling sounds of children laughing, crying, and playing as if the school were still in use. While it's debated whether ghost hunting is a formidable way to tell if a place is haunted, stories abounded about groups who'd catch audio and visual recordings of disembodied voices, shadow figures, and self-emanating balls of light.

Now that the school no longer exists, where have all the ghosts gone? One person said he wonders if the same residual effects are in play today at the recreation center that has since been built in its place.

Magna has its own high school, called Cyprus, and it is rumored to be haunted by prankster ghosts that flick light switches on and off and move the stage curtains of the school's auditorium. Did the spirits who haunted Webster move to the nearby high school? Not likely. The school had been rumored to be haunted for some years previous to Webster's demise.

There are also stories of the mysterious Dead Man's Cave. The Indians, between three thousand and seven thousand years ago, are believed to have used the cave that sits in the mountains in the former town of Garfield, near present-day Magna. It also was used by emigrants passing through the area and early pioneers who eventually settled here. Now owned by Kennecott Copper, the cave is closed to public access. But archeologists who've studied the cave have found layers of refuse from the 1800s and beyond.

In 1952, the cave was fifty-four feet at the mouth, twenty-four feet wide at its rear end, and fifty-nine feet long. The highest point of the cave was only about a foot tall. At one time, according to local historians Lee T. Romrell and Sharon Romrell Staufenbeil in their book *From Mining Town to Ghost Town: A History of Garfield Utah,* there was a small spring to the west of the cave.

Over the years, a lot of mystery has surrounded the cave, later called Dead Man's Cave because rumor had it that a man had committed suicide there. Was it haunted by the man's spirit? "We would try to look for blood on the walls, but never found any," the authors wrote in their book about explorations when the cave was open.

Some people share stories of seeing the spirits of dead men in miner's clothes stalking late-night walkers on the streets of Magna. One story has it that a teenage girl was walking downtown when she spotted an old man beginning to chase her. The girl ran, but kept looking back over her shoulder to see her pursuer gaining on her. And then all of a sudden, he vanished into thin air.

Pleasant Green Cemetery sits on a hill in the southwest quadrant of Magna and overlooks the small township. The bodies of dead miners and family members are buried in the cemetery, as are other people for whom Magna was home. And according to some reports, their spirits have been seen wandering the burial grounds. However, the ghost hunters I've spoken with and certain individuals I met at the cemetery during a visit in March 2011 all say they've never experienced anything paranormal here. A story once was told about green lights seen at night in the cemetery, but it later was determined the glow came from mineral deposits and not anything supernatural.

Restaurant Ghosts

There's at least one ghost that makes her appearance known in a Chinese restaurant in West Jordan, according to a witness who saw the apparition one night while working in the building. He walked around a corner, and there it was—the face and shoulders of a young woman staring at him. Their eyes met, and then the apparition faded from view. The witness said he's never felt anything malevolent in the restaurant, but the encounter startled him.

Apparently, it's not the only eating establishment in the area alleged to be haunted by the spirits of the dead. He's experienced a number of strange and unexplained phenomena while working in the buildings, usually late at night after they've closed. A hamburger joint, for instance, has a ghost that likes to play pranks, turning water faucets on during his cleaning sessions. He doesn't know the connection between the businesses and their spirit guests, but said it has made him more aware of how close this world is to the next.

As far as we know, spirits can't eat. So what is it that makes them haunt restaurants? In other haunts, people have said they've smelled the phantom scent of flowers or perfume. Perhaps ghosts also can smell pleasant aromas. Maybe they visit these restaurants to catch a whiff of the foods they once enjoyed while in mortality. It's as good an explanation as any.

The Spirits of Trolley Square

At about 6:45 on the evening of February 12, 2007, the clatter of casual shopping was shattered by the much louder sounds of gunfire. Sulejman Talovic, an eighteen-year-old Bosnian refugee living in Salt Lake City, entered Trolley Square and began randomly firing at customers and mall employees. Police officers, including an off-duty officer from the Ogden Police Department who was in the mall at the time, shot and killed the assailant, but not before the perpetrator killed five people and wounded several others. Like all violent crime, there was no reason for the senseless tragedy, and it remains unclear what Talovic's motive was for shooting innocent people.

The tragedy has added to the haunted aura of the historic shopping and restaurant complex, not only in a paranormal way, but in the very literal sense that the building now serves as a type of memorial for those who died here. It was never intended as a place for such tragedy.

In 1908, Union Pacific magnate E. H. Harriman selected the site to build a state-of-the-art trolley-car system, which, with 144 trolley cars, served the growing city until the transit line was discontinued in 1945. The mission-style car barns that housed the street cars were in 1972 used to build a two-story shopping center. The building is unique to the area, with its winding hallways, brick and wood floors, and wrought-iron balconies. During the Christmas season, Trolley Square is lit up with festive holiday lights. The center's old-time feel makes just the right atmosphere for a ghost tale or two.

A ghost in bib coveralls presumably has made his appearance more than once at the north doors in the old building, according to security officer Paul Fleming, who wrote a guest column for the October 18, 1999, issue of *The Salt Lake Tribune.*

While on guard duty during a graveyard shift, a maintenance crew worked on the first floor preparing to strip-wax and replace the cobblestone walkway. "It looked liked tedious work," Fleming wrote. "I offered the usual encouraging words before moving upstairs." After making his rounds to make sure every door was locked, Fleming sat down in his office to read a magazine. The night moved slowly, and he was grateful for an interruption at 3:05 A.M., when one of the maintenance men poked his head into the office and asked Fleming to unlock the door so he and his three crew could go grab a bite to eat. Fleming let them out, rebolted the door when they had left, and then surveyed the crew's progress and the haphazardly scattered gear. The work was coming along, Fleming noticed, but the crew still had most of the north corridor to finish.

About an hour later the men knocked on the door to again be let in. No sooner had he opened the door for them when they heard a noise—"an eerie sound that drifted gently through the old car barn," he wrote. One of the men said it sounded like a whistle. Fleming took off to investigate the sound, the work crew trailing behind him. They rounded a bend near the north concourse and stopped. What they saw defied logic and left them puzzling the rest of the night and for days thereafter. "We stared at the scene in front of us and let out a group gasp. The entire length of the corridor had been rewaxed to a glistening buff. Besides that, all of the gear was now stacked neatly against the wall."

The Ghost Woman of the Rio Grande

"Will you marry me?" the man asked the raven-haired woman. They had known each other for some time. "Yes," she said, and all seemed like bliss. And then came the breakup. Like most lore, specific details are lacking, but while the couple was visiting the Rio Grande Depot station in Salt Lake City, they broke into an argument and, in a fit of rage, the man tossed the engagement ring he had purchased for his fianceé onto the tracks. If that didn't end their engagement, the next occurrence did. The woman, not about to lose the ring, jumped onto the tracks to retrieve it—and was struck by an oncoming train. Or so the story goes.

Why the ghost of this woman haunts the women's bathroom at the old depot building is anyone's guess. The facility, now home of the Utah State Historical Society, was built in 1910 by the Rio Grande Western Railroad. The building operated solely as a depot until 1948, but later housed various businesses until the late 1970s, when the historical society purchased the building for a dollar and restored it to its former glory. The only thing lacking today are the trains.

Gravity Hill

It's a fact of science: what goes up must come down—unless you're parked on Gravity Hill, where things that are down slowly go up. At least that's what appears to happen on a street northeast of the Utah State Capitol Building in Salt Lake City, where, if you park your vehicle on the hill and put it in the neutral position, it will begin to slowly ascend the hill.

A number of other states apparently have their own gravity hills, and like Utah's famous road, they become the talk of the town. As if the very real phenomena isn't strange enough, one of the stories associated with Utah's Gravity Hill claims that Emo's spirit, whose gravesite allegedly glows blue at night and lies not far from the hill (see page 38), somehow warps gravity in the area and causes the phenomena. Another story says a farmer was killed when the tractor he was driving up the hill couldn't make it and rolled. Intent in making sure others make it up the hill, the farmer's ghost energy pulls the stationary vehicles.

In truth, the explanation isn't as paranormal as some might think. It's really an optical illusion. The car actually is descending, but because of the layout of the surrounding hillsides—which seem to grow taller as you descend—it appears as if you are really moving up.

Gravity Hill is a popular destination for teenagers, who like to frighten their dates with the phenomena and the tall tales behind it. And as you can see, the scientific explanation isn't nearly as fun as believing that spirit energies are at work on the hill. After all, it's not every day that your car gets driven by a ghost.

Want to experience Gravity Hill yourself? Drive a few blocks northeast of the Utah State Capitol to Bonneville Boulevard, which loops around Memory Grove in lower City Creek Canyon. Be careful and don't stop long: Gravity Hill is a public road. Make sure your vehicle's headlights and hazard lights are turned on at night.

Talking Tree Cemetery

Visit just about any cemetery at night and you're likely to experience weirdness, whether it's your imagination or something more paranormal. Visit the Highland City Cemetery, for instance, and you might be able to hear the spirits of the dead try to communicate with you.

As the legend goes, if you sit on a certain bench in the cemetery at night a light wind will kick up. Listen closely, and what you'll hear will be more than the rustling of leaves. The voices of spirits apparently carry on the wind and become more pronounced by the wind's interaction with the trees.

This is a nice story, but likely isn't true. It doesn't take much imagination to hear ghostly sounds whenever wind blows through trees, causing leaves to shimmer and boughs to bend.

Or is there more to the story? Like most legends, myth is born of some truth.

The Ghosts of Copperton

There's something unique about the Oquirrh Mountains. You can't help but notice the flat-topped, volcano-looking copper mines in the range's middle-south section. These are the largest open-pit copper mines in the world. Now owned by Kennecott Copper, the site didn't start out producing copper at all. Prospectors first sought gold from the ore-heavy mountains.

The U.S. Army first claimed the site in 1863, when soldiers, who doubled as prospectors, scoured the mountain range and claimed the site as their own. But it was the Bingham brothers, Thomas and Sandford, who first knew about the site's rich ore supply. While grazing cattle in the area in the 1850s, they noticed deposits in the ground. Not knowing what they should do, they approached Brigham Young, who told them to leave it alone for fear of attracting outsiders. His ambition was thwarted when U.S. soldiers arrived and began prospecting the mountains. Before long, dozens of mining camps dotted the area. Lead and silver were the primary metals extracted from the mines, with small traces of gold. It later was discovered that the copper being extracted with the other metals was in much larger quantities, which was worth more than the small amounts of gold being retrieved. That changed the miners' focus and their primary efforts soon went to extracting copper. The Utah Copper Company (now Kennecott Copper) was formed in 1903, driving more people to the area.

Bingham Canyon continued to grow in popularity and population. By the 1920s, it is estimated that more than fifteen thousand people lived in the canyon. A decade later, though, mining was becoming a much bigger beast, and it began to push residents from their homes as the operation expanded. A smelter established in 1906 in Garfield at the north end of the mountain near the Great Salt Lake grew its own town, but Bingham City was dying. Residents moved away. By 1961, Bingham City was gone. But like a haunting, residue of the past remains.

Copperton, a small community that in almost every way looks and feels old, still exists not far from Bingham Canyon. Old-style homes, tall shade trees, a cozy park, a gothic-looking church, the site of a now-razed school, and a lonely cemetery are the hallmarks of Copperton. A few newer homes, a post office, and a fire station also make their home here, but it's the old houses, buildings, and trees that give the community its charm. And like any historic community, it has its ghosts.

I remember stories about the Old Bingham City Cemetery. When I was attending Bingham Middle School, there was a long-haired kid who was a class reject, a loner. I didn't know him, only knew about him, and I felt sorry for the teenage boy. I tried talking with him once, but he didn't seem to like the company. Then one day I heard the rumor. The boy was a devil worshipper. He had told a group of students one day during gym class that he was going to walk to the nearby cemetery after school, pronounce a curse upon some of the students, and commit suicide by smashing his head against a gravestone. I don't think the kid ever followed through with his intended suicide, as I saw him a day or two later at school and several more times that year. There were stories like that back when I went to school at BMS in the 1980s. And there were also stories of ghosts that haunted the then-decrepit looking graveyard.

A number of the cemetery's headstones are nameless, the inscriptions having worn off over decades of harsh winters and hot summers. What are the names of the people who lie beneath the stones? Was it these spirits that haunted the grounds, wishing to make themselves known to those mortals who visited?

The cemetery is now owned by the Jordan School District, and over the past several years Boy Scouts and other groups have helped to better care for the burial yard. In 2008, a group comprising various businesses and service organizations erected a veterans' memorial at the cemetery, honoring those who served in conflicts as far back as the Civil War. And still, the ghosts live on.

I remember the school well: old brick façade, large windows, broad hallways, multiple levels, spacious classrooms, and, in the boys' locker room, dried blood on the wall furnace. And always the same musty chalkboard smell. The smell at times made me nauseous, while the blood frightened me. How did the blood get there? Had there been a fight? And, most unnerving, why wasn't it ever cleaned up? Rumor had it that the school had seen a lot of blood during its ninety-four-year history, blood from bleeding noses caused by fistfights. Stories about the fights were just some of the tales that caused young minds to wander. The other stories were of spectral classmates who, when I attended, seemed to still roam the expansive facility. Whether because of the stories or because of its age—by the 1980s the building seemed to show its every wrinkle—there was something creepy about the 1908-built schoolhouse.

As with people, the years had caught up with the school. Rather than spend money to renovate the existing building, it was determined by 1994 that a wiser course would be to build a new school. That November, the Jordan Board of Education approved a land trade-purchase to acquire property to build a new middle school in South Jordan, a growing modern community about seven miles to the east. Bingham Middle School still functioned until 1996, but then closed its doors. It sat empty for a few years except for the trespassers who sneaked their way onto the property to explore its tunneled depths.

Dead Places, a group that explores old buildings, ventured inside the schoolhouse more than once starting in February 2000 and claimed to have found a nuclear fallout shelter, maps of mine tunnels, spent bullet shells, and a noose hanging in a former art room. It was rumored at the time that the school was a secret training facility for law enforcement where they prepared for a school emergency.

Rumor said there were spirits of former students that walked the empty hallways, and that the sounds of laughter and student commotion could be heard in the classrooms. People would feel eyes watching them and hear unearthly noises deep inside the old building.

The school was demolished in 2002. It made me sad. When I last visited the old school grounds, green grass had taken over where the brown building once stood. But standing alone, as if reaching for something unseen by human eyes, was a set of stairs—a stairway to an ethereal world where the school and its ghosts now exist.

Utah Valley
and Beyond

THE STATE'S LARGEST FRESHWATER BODY, UTAH LAKE, LIES in Utah
Valley, as does one of the country's largest privately owned univer-
sities. The area is bordered by rugged mountains to the east and
open space to the west, where sits the lake, giving it a tranquil setting. But looks can be deceiving, for even amid its tranquility are
things that go bump in the night. In some cases, it's more than a
bump—like the Phantom Hitchhiker of American Fork, the strange
goings-on at a former hospital, the ghostly outdoorsman who likes
to walk with hikers, and the strange, unexplained lights that have
been seen hovering over the valley.

The Phantom Hitchhiker of American Fork

Not unlike Marley's ghost who was forever destined to carry chains
in the afterlife in Charles Dickens's timeless tale *A Christmas Carol*,
some ghosts seem forever destined to wander the earth without
ever going anywhere. Such is the case with the Phantom Hitchhiker
of American Fork Canyon. We don't really know to whom this ghost
belongs, but he must enjoy the outdoors because almost anything
you've ever wanted to do outdoors is available to do in the canyon.

Fishermen love American Fork Canyon, located in the Uinta National Forest, about forty-five minutes southeast of Salt Lake City. A popular place to drown a worm is Tibble Fork Lake, a reservoir that is fed by two rivers that begin high in the Unita Mountains. Farther up the canyon is Silver Lake Flats. Both waters are stocked with rainbow trout, but anglers have been known to pull brook, brown, and cutthroat trout from the waters. If fishing isn't your thing, you can hike up 11,750-foot Mount Timpanogos, visit pleasant Cascade Springs, or take a leisurely drive through scenic Alpine Loop. There also are trails for hiking, horseback or off-road riding, and cozy campsites and picnic spots near babbling rivers. One camping area above Tibble Fork even has a softball field. The canyon is prettiest in fall, but busiest in summer, when anglers dot the shores and sunbathers lie beneath a warm sky. A variety of trees, wildflowers, birds, and animals make their homes here. Moose have been known to wander amid the thick trees, near the stream or close to the road.

Sounds like a nice place, right? It is. And if you're here at night, you just might see a ghost. With thumb sticking out, this phantom is looking for a ride. According to local lore, the person to whom this ghost belongs was the victim of an accidental death that occurred in the canyon long ago, and he's been looking for a ride home ever since. He must not be too serious about leaving the canyon, though, for if you stop to pick him up, he quickly vanishes.

American Fork Canyon is a nice place to hang out, and this ghostly hitchhiker isn't the only specter said to haunt the area. A number of apparitions, light anomalies, and phantom noises have been reported here. Phantom screams have reportedly been heard emanating throughout the canyon.

The Heart of Timpanogos

Her dark eyes flitted, catching the young brave's attention. Then he noticed her soft face and gentle skin, and something moved inside him. Ucanogos felt a fluttering in her own stomach as she thought about the handsome Timpanac. A courtship began. Though they came from different tribes, perhaps the Great Spirit would unite them in marriage.

But Timpanac, as the story goes, wasn't the only young man who vied for Ucanogos. Other braves who lived in the shadow of the Wasatch Mountains wanted her heart's affection, so an Indian chief, supposedly Ucanogos's father, proposed a contest. The young braves were to kill an animal with their bare hands, race around a lake, and climb to the top of a mountain peak. The winner, who'd demonstrate his bravery, stamina, and skill, would be gifted Ucanogos as his bride.

The race began and much to Ucanogos's delight, Timpanac proved fit for the challenge. It looked as if the Great Spirit would grant them their wish. But when Timpanac climbed the mountain for the final feat, his fellow competitors, not willing to be bested, wrestled the young brave down and threw him off a cliff. When word reached Ucanogos that her Timpanac had been killed, she was so distraught that she climbed the mountain herself and leaped to her death to join her heartthrob in eternity.

There are different versions of the alleged Ute story, but all have the same ending: the two lovers die, their spirits unite in death, and their hearts meld together as a heart-shaped stalactite inside Utah's most popular cave, Timpanogos, named for the two Indian lovers. Some believe the story isn't an Indian folktale at all, but was created by Eugene Lusk "Timp" Roberts, a professor at Brigham Young University, who in the early 1900s made up the story in an effort to promote the mountain as a tourist destination.

There is a heart-shaped stalactite inside one of the caves at Mount Timpanogos. The mountain, which stretches through Provo, Orem, Pleasant Grove, and American Fork, includes three natural caves that contain at least forty-two types of differing rock formations. Visitors can access a hiking trail near a visitor's center in American Fork Canyon. The mile-and-a-half trail is a steep hike, climbing to an elevation of more than one thousand feet, so it's important that hikers are in good health. The cave is open from about mid-May to mid-October. There's a nominal fee to enter the canyon, where you can see the famous heart-shaped stalactite that perhaps has a history like no other.

Strange Lights over Utah County

When it comes to strange phenomena, perhaps nothing triggers the imagination as much as the topic of unidentified flying objects. Some people laugh at stories about UFOs, while others who are not as skeptical wonder about the great plan of life. If there's life on Earth, they wonder, could there be life elsewhere? Are we the only intelligent creatures to inhabit the expansive universe and its many galaxies? Will we ever know?

As night fell on January 26, 2011, people in Utah Valley grabbed their cameras, video recorders, and cell phones to capture strange lights in the sky. The three red lights, attached to an unknown craft, appeared stationary for about fifteen minutes in the sky near American Fork and Highland before flying away. While hovering, the craft dropped white, flare-like lights that blinked out before hitting the ground. Area news teams quickly jumped on the story in an effort to find the source of the lights.

"They looked like they were flying perfectly in formation together, and whatever was dropping was burning real bright," Mike Galbraith, an eyewitness, told local news station ABC4. People tried to come up with explanations for the strange incident. Were the lights attached to helicopters? No sound. Maybe hot air balloons? Military and airport officials offered no explanation for the lights, confirming they did not have any training or other activities scheduled that night.

With the lack of official evidence, the sighting left some people wondering if Utah received a close encounter of another kind. For now, the case is filed under "unidentified." Interestingly, the Utah incident occurred just two nights before sightings were reported of similar lights over the Dome of the Rock in Jerusalem.

Hiking with Ghosts?

It's always more fun to hike with someone than to go alone. You might change your tune, however, if your companion is a ghost. And that is who your companion just might be at Rock Canyon, a popular hiking venue east of Utah Lake near the Oak Hills. Lore has it that the place is haunted by the spirits of people who died from hiking or other disasters in the canyon. The Associated Press, for instance, reported on October 11, 2006, that a thirty-year-old man named Brian Eggett fell four hundred feet to his death while hiking to the top of Squaw Peak. Interestingly, the peak was named after an Indian squaw who fell to her death while climbing the cliff in the 1850s. Police said the man's death was an accident. It's believed the squaw's death was also accidental. She apparently was fleeing a band of Mormon militiamen, who for several days had battled with her tribe along the Provo River.

It was a time of conflict for the Indians, who had inhabited the land for centuries, and the newcomer Mormons, who began to settle the valley in the middle 1800s. The Indians didn't like the white man taking over, and it often led to skirmishes between the two groups. One conflict came to a head in 1850 along the Provo River, where a battle raged for several days between about seventy Indians led by Big Elk and members of the Mormon militia. Many Indians were hurt or killed in the battle, and the remaining group eventually fled; some headed south, and others, including Big Elk, escaped to Rock Canyon. Big Elk, having sustained wounds in the conflict, died at the mouth of the canyon. Later, when his squaw saw the militiamen approach, she allegedly tried climbing a cliff but fell.

Other accidents have occurred in the canyon. Evidence of satanic rituals and the bodies of murder victims also have allegedly been found here, which spawned further rumor about the site being haunted. One story has it that the shade of a man dressed in 1970s garb is sometimes seen standing on one of the rock peaks before running or gliding down at high speed. People have reported hearing strange, unexplained noises in the canyon and experiencing unnerving feelings of being followed.

The canyon was the topic of discussion by neighbors in late March 2009, but it had nothing to do with the paranormal. Residents of the area had gathered to protest Richard Davis, the owner of an old mining claim, who according to the *Daily Herald* wanted to "quarry one side of the iconic quartzite rock 'gates' that flank the canyon mouth." Neighbors wanted to keep the quiet nature of the environment intact, without the ruckus of mine work.

The trail is best hiked during the summer months, as it can be snow-covered from October to late spring. Just keep an eye out for your ghostly hiking companions.

Utah Lake's Black-Eyed Monster

Lake monsters were all the rage in Utah in the mid- to late-1800s. You've read about the Bear Lake Monster, but that was only one of five alleged monsters in as many Utah lakes.

The second-most famous monster was one rumored to haunt Utah Lake. The serpent-like creature was reported to have an elongated neck and piercing black eyes. An early report of the monster surfaced in August 1868, when Lehi resident Henry Walker reported that while on the lake four years previous he saw what appeared to be "a large snake . . . with the head of a greyhound," D. Robert Carter, a historian and former schoolteacher, was reported as saying in the *Deseret News* on September 23, 2001. Two other men reported a similar sighting in the Jordan River, the lake's only outlet, noting that it had "wicked-looking black eyes."

Utah Lake, at about 145 square miles, is the state's largest freshwater body. It now is a state park, but once was part of ancient Lake Bonneville. Some believed the monster was an inhabitant of the ancient lake. The Jordan River, so named because of its similar topography to the same-named river in Israel that flows from the Sea of Galilee to the Dead Sea, runs to its own dead sea, the Great Salt Lake, where another monster reportedly lived long ago. The other Utah lakes where monsters were reported to live include Bear Lake in northern Utah, Sevier Lake in west-central Utah, and Panguitch Lake in south-central Utah. It later was reported that Moon Lake in northeastern Utah was inhabited by a monster as well.

A few reports similar to Walker's surfaced during the same time period, but nothing was ever officially documented. According to the *Deseret News*, lake monsters were "fashionable" in the early 1870s, but by the next decade had "fallen out of favor."

"There was one sighting and a brief upsurge in 1921 for the Utah Lake monster, but then it 'sank in the depths of the lake' and apparently hasn't been seen since," the paper reported.

Bridal Veil Falls

"These violent delights have violent ends," wrote Shakespeare. "And in their triumph die, like fire and powder/Which as they kiss consume." The famous playwright haunted audiences with his tragedy, *Romeo and Juliette*.

The ghost of a woman who died much like Juliette is said to haunt Bridal Veil Falls in Provo Canyon. An Indian maiden long ago was betrothed to be married to her chosen lover, but on the very day she was supposed to become his bride, she heard that he had been killed. Overcome with grief at losing the love of her life, the young maiden climbed to the top of a mountain and flung herself from the cliffs. As it turned out, the young man hadn't died after all. When he found out what his bride had done, his heart became very heavy. There are different variations of the story, but all have similar endings that give reasons why Bridal Veil Falls might be haunted.

Stories have sprung up over the years about phantom cries that are heard in the canyon and the shade of an Indian woman that often has been seen walking the roadsides.

The falls, once a stop along the route of the Heber Creeper tourist train, is a scenic spot along U.S. Highway 189. The 607-foot, double-cataract waterfall has attracted locals and passersby for years and is still a popular stopping spot for those traveling on the highway. The site was first owned by Utah senator Rue Clegg, who acquired the land in 1929. It changed hands over the years until 1971, when an Orem family by the name of Grown acquired the property.

Bridal Veil Falls at one time featured a tram that would take visitors up the mountainside to a restaurant and overlook perched on the cliffs. Both the building and tram no longer exist, having been destroyed by avalanches and fires, though over the years there's been a push by some folks to rebuild the tram. But during its heyday rumors had it that the restaurant allegedly was haunted. People would report seeing dark shades and objects move.

If you plan to visit Bridal Veil Falls, don't be surprised if you happen to see the ghostly shade of a hitchhiker, as that's another story about the canyon.

A Former Haunt in Lehi

Hospitals are the perfect setting to tell a ghost story. Stephen King knew this when he wrote a thirteen-part teleplay called *Kingdom Hospital*, based on Lars von Trier's *The Kingdom*, that aired on ABC from March to July 2004. The concept was correct, even if the story was a little goofy. What other places besides hospitals have hosted so much physical and emotional trauma, illness, and death?

Long before King's miniseries aired, there were reports of ghostly shades, phantom voices, and other paranormal occurrences at a now-razed hospital in Lehi. The only difference between these stories and the one that King told is that these stories allegedly are true.

It starts with a doctor who went over the edge one night and killed his nurse by stringing her up from the hospital's flag pole. The tale to me sounds like an urban legend, and I could not find any records to document its truthfulness. There was something unnerving about the building, however, for paranormal investigators who spent some time in the hospital. They reported capturing a number of voice recordings, many from entities that seem to express being lost in the building or warnings to their human visitors to "get out." Besides serving as a hospital, the building at one time played host to a church and crematorium, which might further explain why the building was rumored to be haunted.

The building was constructed in 1891 as a bank, with its upper-floor rooms used for LDS church services. The basement supposedly at one time housed the county's crematorium. It became a hospital in 1921 and served in that capacity until 1968, when Lehi built a larger, more modern facility to better serve the needs of the growing community. Eventually the old building was used as a Halloween attraction in the 1980s, which, with a story like the hanged nurse, seems to have been a fitting site for a spook house. Over the years the building also was used as a ballroom, photo studio, and school. It was finally vacated in 1989.

Were the stories, such as the one about the deranged doctor hanging the nurse, created to attract visitors to the Halloween event or were they based on fact? It's likely that some of the stories were fiction, but perhaps not all. Various web postings indicate a number of people believe the old hospital was home to patients whose spirits, once they crossed over for one reason or another, couldn't manage to leave. It was even rumored that the spirit of the dead nurse was seen walking around the spot of her mortal demise.

The building was a favorite spot for area ghost hunters, who captured audio recordings of phantom voices, including some who seemed to say they were lost in the building, and visual recordings of shadow movement.

Too bad the hospital isn't around anymore, as investigators likely would still be scouring the premises searching for an explanation of the unknown. The building, which had been a fixture in Lehi for decades, was demolished in March 2009.

The Weeping Lady of Spanish Fork

For the living, cemeteries are sacred places of reflection, places of tribute. They sometimes bring out our deepest emotions as we visit the burial site of loved ones who've gone on before. It's only natural that a person might cry while visiting a cemetery. What is not natural is a statue that can cry, but that supposedly is what happens at the Spanish Fork City Cemetery.

"Eternally carved in stone, the weeping lady has been kneeling over the grave site of Laura Daniels Ferreday of Payson since Ferreday died in 1929," Rodger L. Hardy wrote in an article published October 18, 2005, in the *Deseret News*. "One hand of the weeping lady presses against a wall, her face buried in her other arm. Ferreday's husband, Horace, was laid to rest beside her in 1972." City records show that Laura Ferreday, then thirty-two, died in 1929 in Provo of an infectious tumor, according to the article.

Today if you walk around the cemetery with your eyes closed, you'll be able to hear the carved lady weep. Some even claim the watermarks you see near her face are from actual tears.

The legend about the weeping lady has been around for decades, perhaps spurred by adventurous teenagers who took their dates to the cemetery in an effort to scare them into their arms. Stories about weeping-lady statues are common in many states; some states, including Utah, have more than one. For instance, there's a statue of a kneeling woman, her forehead buried in one hand, at the Logan City Cemetery that cries for dead children. If you sit in front of the statue during a full moon, as the legend goes, you can see tears come from the statue's eyes.

As for the legend of the weeping lady of Spanish Fork, resident Tim Moran said there's nothing to it. Moran lived across from the cemetery for more than forty years and knew Horace Ferreday as a child, according to the *Deseret News* article. He said the only thing he ever heard was "the nighttime screaming of teenagers who go in there to play."

Question: Did he ever walk the cemetery at night with his eyes closed?

The White Lady of Spring Canyon

The funny thing about some stories is how they get embellished and enriched over the years. But even tall tales have some truth to them. The truth behind the story about the White Lady of Spring Canyon, also known as the White Lady of Latuda, rumored to haunt an old mining camp near Helper, is difficult to tell because this story actually has many variations.

To understand any of them, you first must know a little about Spring Canyon, a once-bustling mining site in Carbon County that was home to a number of different communities that rose in the late 1800s and early 1900s. Not much is left in the canyon today, except an historic imprint of what used to be in the wilds of rural Utah.

The canyon began to be developed around 1895, but grew by leaps and bounds beginning in about 1912, when Jesse Knight purchased sixteen hundred acres and started the Spring Canyon Coal Company. Here he built homes for the workers and a year later, in 1913, he constructed a railroad to connect with the Denver and Rio Grande lines in nearby Helper. Within a year, more than one thousand tons of coal was being mined from the canyon every day. Its success continued for the next forty years, eventually increasing production to around two thousand tons a day during World War II. Besides the homes that Knight had built, there also arose a hotel, church, and school. The town's success didn't last, however, and eventually the mines began to dwindle. So did the communities, as people began to leave. At one time Spring Canyon was home to more than two thousand people, but by 1969 the mines had closed. Besides a few buildings and a railroad trestle, what's left is the White Lady.

"Though the mine brought people and prosperity to the region, it also brought tragedy and violence in mining explosions and major strikes," writes Kathy Weiser on the *Legends of America* website. "But, when Spring Canyon's heydays were over, it left behind only memories, scattered mining remnants, fading ghost towns, and legends, the most famous of which is that of the White Lady."

As mentioned previously, there are many variations to the story. A young lady whom we'll call Mary was widowed when her husband was killed in a mine disaster in the early 1900s. His body was never found, causing Mary, now herself a ghost, to wander the canyon in search of her beloved. Another story has it that if miners followed Mary into the mines, disaster would befall them. Still another story has it that Mary would entice men to leave the mines to avoid disaster. All of the stories have one thing in common: Mary is known to appear in a white gown or dress.

Perhaps the most popular story is this one: The woman's husband died, leaving her and their two children with little economic means. She didn't want her babies to starve because she could not afford to buy any food. She went to the Latuda mine office for financial help, but was given none. In a desperate moment, she killed her children by drowning them in a nearby creek. The woman supposedly checked herself into a psychiatric hospital in Salt Lake City, but later returned to the canyon, where she hanged herself. Since then, her ghost has been seen by a number of visitors. Strange lights, sometimes green in color, also have been reported in the area.

Military Ghosts at Camp Floyd

Camp Floyd at one time was the temporary home to thousands of U.S. soldiers. Remnants of the old barracks site, now known as the Camp Floyd/Stagecoach Inn State Park, sit in the small town of Fairfield about twenty-two miles west of Lehi. The camp once comprised nearly four hundred buildings, but all that remains today is the commissary building, schoolhouse, and cemetery.

The camp was constructed in 1858 when President James Buchanan sent Col. Albert Sidney Johnston to Utah Territory with a force of three thousand federal soldiers to quell a feared uprising by the Mormons. The Latter-day Saints had arrived in Utah the decade before and tried to establish their own sovereign state. But relations between the church and federal government were contentious. Since the troops would be staying for an extended period of time, Johnston searched for a spot to build a permanent camp. He chose Fairfield, which five years earlier had been scouted by Amos Fielding and was known for its pleasant springs.

The camp, which Johnston named after then secretary of war John B. Floyd, included a 1,600-by-300-foot wall with a gate that opened into Fairfield, as well as barracks, a commissary building, a schoolhouse, and nearly four hundred other buildings. When completed, it was deemed the largest military camp in the West.

Interestingly, though the camp was constructed as a place for soldiers to keep watch over the Mormons, it was essentially the Mormons who were hired to build the complex. Materials to construct the fort came locally, some even from church-owned mills. The camp would serve its intended purpose for only a short period, however. The anticipated "Utah War" between the Latter-day Saints and federal government never materialized, and in hindsight, it was more like a "cold war" than anything else. By 1861, with its focus turned to an impending civil war, the Army packed up, dismantled most of the buildings, and left the camp.

The park today is state-owned and in the summer of 2011 was working with the Veterans Administration towards establishing markers for the site's known graves, said park manager Mark Trotters. Ground-penetrating radar had been used to pinpoint burial sites and it was discovered that headstones were in locations where no graves were previously found. As for the other mysteries of the park, Trotters allowed paranormal groups to investigate after volunteers and staff reported odd occurrences, such as unseen forces tugging on doors and a dress that appeared to float in midair.

The Utah Ghost Hunters Society investigated the park in 2005, according to an October 31, 2005, article by *Deseret News* writer Jared Page. Society member Nancy Peterson told Page the group had previously collected EVPs at the cemetery, including intelligent interaction with an entity that said his name was Bryan. "But I'm dead," Bryan told the group.

When I called Trotters on May 18, 2011, he deferred comment about the investigations to Joshua Bryant, an investigator with the Cache Paranormal Research Society.

"It is definitely a highly active place," Bryant told me, noting that he too has experienced intelligent interaction with spirits at the camp. "A little kid comes talking over the top of us, not echoey and fuzzy like an EVP, but clear and full-bodied, and says, 'Hey, are you guys in there.' Like he could hear us in there, but couldn't see us."

Most hauntings in Utah, including those at Camp Floyd, are residual in nature, Bryant said. Only about ten percent are intelligent hauntings. But, he notes, his group is "pushing the envelope" on residual theories. "As far as residual stuff goes, a lot of the time you can actually be getting intelligent residual activity; it's not picking up another time or energy current that's on this place but more one that lapses over our current time as we understand it."

"We don't know," Bryant continued. "We think there are places where the veil that lets us see their world and lets them see into our world is thinner. A lot of those places are vortexes, and that's something paranormal investigators have went off of for a long time with electromagnetic-field detectors and things like that; like places that have a high electromagnetic field might be likely to conduct more activity. We actually want to try to develop equipment that can actually detect proton activity, which basically is a modified Geiger counter. . . . We honestly believe there's a lot to do with that, with protons and tachyons and things like that. Basically energy that travels backward and forward through space and time without any regard for any of what we consider to be dimensions."

Camp Floyd seems to have a mixture of intelligent and what is considered "traditional" residual hauntings. Phantom footsteps in the old commissary building have been heard as well as what seems to be the chattering of men in conversation; lights have been known to turn on and off, and at least once a piano thought to be broken started playing. Shadow figures also have been reported.

If you wish to visit the old military camp, Bryant said you have nothing to worry about. The group has never encountered anything malevolent at the camp. "It's haunted with the history of the place," he said. "Places like that are going to absorb the activity."

The Ghosts of Santaquin

If you were to search place names, you'd find many interesting stories as to how and why locations received their monikers. Santaquin is one place in the Beehive State with an interesting name history.

When a Ute Indian was killed near Springville, Chief Wakara demanded to know which Mormon had killed the Indian brave. When his request was denied, he initiated raids on Mormon settlements. Fearing for their safety, the band of pioneers who settled Summit City in 1851 had by 1853 (when the raids began) fled their growing township. The group moved to nearby Payson, where Mormon numbers were larger, and didn't return to their former precinct until two years later.

Then one night after they returned, Benjamin F. Johnson, a prominent figure among the pioneer group, was visited by his friend Chief Guffich, a Ute friendly to the Mormons. He warned Johnson that a raiding party was making plans to attack the town. Heeding his friend's warning, Johnson again led his group of pioneers to Payson. When the raiding party, which included Guffich's son Santaquin, found the fort deserted, Guffich told them that the white men were good people and that the Great Spirit had warned them to leave. This appeased the would-be attackers. The pioneers returned and, thankful for the chief's warning, suggested the city be named Guffich. But the Indian chief declined the honor, asking instead that it be named after his son, Santaquin.

Santaquin today is a cozy community with a population of more than eight thousand, according to 2008 estimates. It offers a picturesque view of Utah Lake and Mount Timpanogos, and it has a few ghosts. People who've visited the nearby canyon say they've felt cold spots, heard strange noises, and seen unexplained, self-illuminating lights. Others have walked away with unnerving feelings of being watched or followed. In the city itself, there've been reports by some residents who claim to have seen apparitions in their homes. Moving objects and loud, phantom noises also have been reported to occur in at least one restaurant.

Northeastern Utah

ABOUT FORTY-FIVE MINUTES EAST OF SALT LAKE CITY IS ICONIC PARK City, a former mining town now known for its eclectic retail stores and restaurants, festivals, and winter sports attractions. Farther east and north are the scenic dinosaur lands, where life is more rural, the scenery more rugged and lonely. It is in these areas, Park City and beyond, where our focus now lies. For among the beauty of northeastern Utah, there are stories about alien spooks, strange creatures, and freaky ghosts.

The Ghostly Miners of Park City

Over the past several years there've been a number of news reports about accidents in mines—workers becoming trapped and, in some instances, losing their lives because of their injuries or because they couldn't escape the collapse. Perhaps the best-known mine disaster in recent memory is the one that happened on August 5, 2010, in northern Chile's Atacama Desert. Thirty-three miners became trapped twenty-three hundred feet below the Earth's surface because of a cave-in at the copper and gold mine. Rescue personnel worked for weeks in an attempt to help the trapped miners. Just as the would-be rescuers decided the miners couldn't still be alive, a note scrawled in red and taped to a drill bit was retrieved. "Estamos bien en el refugio, los 33," the note read. "We are well in the shelter, the 33." This good news fortified the rescuers who worked tirelessly to reach the miners. Rescue attempts continued for the next sixty-two days before the miners were reached. Loved ones stood by, anxious to hear the report. They feared the miners were dead. Miraculously, all had survived.

Unfortunately, not every mine disaster ends with good news. Just four years before, on January 2, 2006, thirteen miners became trapped underground after an explosion at the Sago Mine in West Virginia. Rescuers reached the miners two days later; only one miner was found alive. In today's world of advanced technology it might seem old-fashioned to have men toiling in holes deep in the ground, but mining has played an important role in American history, and, closer to home, Utah history. In the late 1800s, it played a crucial role in forming the area now known as Park City.

Park City, a scenic resort town nestled in Summit and Wasatch counties, is one of Utah's most popular destination spots. Its famous ski resorts attract thousands of visitors every year and played host to some of the events during the 2002 Salt Lake Olympic Winter Games. But there's plenty to do in this highbrow community long before the snow flies, and other things to do besides skiing when it does. One attraction is hot-air balloon rides. For the price of a ticket, visitors can climb the skies to view the mountainous landscape from a bird's perspective. Those who do are impressed with the picturesque view, though they might not know about the city's troubled past and its dark, recessed silver mines.

In about 1868, prospectors began searching the mountains in Park City. They previously had mined areas along the Wasatch Front and in the Oquirrh range to the west. In the Oquirrhs, they found rich deposits of copper, but in the area now known as Park City they found beds of silver and lead. By December 1868, the first mining claim was filed in the city; over the ensuing years a number of mining operations began, and before long Park City became a bustling community. But such good fortune didn't last long before tragedy struck the growing mining town. Fires in 1882 and 1885 and a particularly bad fire in 1898 caused havoc to the miners, residents, and businesses. After the 1898 fire, which had destroyed Main Street and left the town in ruins, residents banded together to rebuild the community. By 1920, Park City had been rebuilt, retaining its nineteenth-century mining-town look. "This look," according to Utah.com, "is part of the attraction that draws visitors to Park City." Some, however, have come to explore the mines where it is reported the phantom voices of the miners are still heard today.

Mystery of the Skinwalker

Strange lights in the sky, cattle mutilations, and creatures with yellow eyes are just some of the stories associated with Skinwalker Ranch, a 480-acre parcel in the scenic Uinta Basin. The ranch has been talked about for years in the same vein as Nevada's Area 51, because of the unearthly phenomena that allegedly has been witnessed at the rural site.

Stories about the ranch, which sits near an Indian reservation in the expansive rough of nature between Roosevelt and Vernal, go back several years. Local Indians believe the area is haunted by what the Ute and Navajo Indians call "Skinwalkers," shape-shifting creatures that are able to pass between our world and the dimensions beyond. Stories purportedly told by hundreds of witnesses over the years have to do with Bigfoot-like creatures, mysterious flying orbs, bulletproof wolves, and poltergeist activity.

The stories received new attention when George A. Knapp produced a series of articles about the strange goings-on at the ranch for the now-defunct *Las Vegas Mercury*. He later co-authored with Colm A. Kelleher *Hunt for the Skinwalker: Science Confronts the Unexplained at a Remote Ranch in Utah*. The book details the experiences of Tom and Ellen Gorman, who at one time lived at the ranch and experienced a number of frightening encounters with strange creatures, poltergeists, and unidentified flying objects, including a hovering triangular craft that was seen floating over fields.

In 1996 the property was acquired by a paranormal research group known as the National Institute for Discovery Science to study anecdotal reports of strange phenomena. During Knapp and Kelleher's stay at the ranch they investigated nearly one hundred leads of unexplained phenomena.

Stories about UFOs have circulated in the Uinta Basin since at least the 1950s. By some estimates, according to the authors, more than half of the basin's residents have seen anomalous objects in the sky. During the 1960s and '70s, the Utah Highway Patrol received so many reports about UFO sightings that the department stopped following up on them. Junior Hicks, a local UFO historian, collected more than four hundred stories of UFO sightings that had occurred in the basin. Hicks even shared a personal experience that occurred in the '70s, when he "watched an orange ball fly over the town of Roosevelt at a high rate of speed, then make an abrupt right-angle turn. The ball hovered in the air over the town before zipping out of sight at an incredible speed. In at least six of the cases he investigated, witnesses say they saw not only the spaceships but also the occupants of the craft." One rancher described a ship's occupants as "wearing white coveralls."

What is it about the Uinta Basin that sparks such frightening experiences? If there are such things as otherworldly beings, what interest do they have in a small ranch in rural Utah? Some believe the stories are exaggerated, that such things as cattle mutilations and crop circles are easily explained as the work of pranksters; others believe the ranch is now a government site used for secret military purposes. People have reported that armed military personnel will show up if you get too close. Interestingly, a note at the end of one of Knapp's newspaper articles reads, "Warning to paranormal enthusiasts: Do not travel to the ranch. You are not welcome there. It is private property and the people who live on or near it don't want to be hassled by curiosity seekers or the media." It ends by saying the level of unexplained phenomena has declined, "so chances are you wouldn't see anything even if you could get on the property."

Little Vicki

It started as just another day for Shannon Giles, a ranger with the Ashley National Forest. He was using a blower to sweep leaves and other debris from one of the campsites, when out of nowhere he heard a voice. "Daddy," it said as clear as day, a whisper in his ear. He stopped the blower, looked around, and didn't see anyone. He was the only one at the Moon Lake campsite. It surprised him, but he didn't think much about it until several days later when he started hearing similar stories from others. People reported that they, too, heard the phantom voice of a little girl. The voice had

startled campers out of their tents. "Help me," it pleaded, sometimes rattling the canvas, "I'm cold." The campers, thinking a child needed their help, would climb from their tents in search of the voice. But, like Giles, they'd find no one. Other people actually claimed to have seen the apparition of a little girl, no older than eight years old. She never sticks around for long, because once her image has been seen it slowly vanishes. Whoever the ghost girl is, she apparently was the victim of a drowning, because when she appears she looks like she's wet.

But that is in itself a mystery, Giles said. In all his research of Moon Lake, he's never uncovered a story about a young girl who drowned here. But because so many claim to have heard or seen her, they've given her a name. They call her Little Vicki. Giles said stories about Little Vicki have been circulated since the turn of the last century.

Little Vicki apparently likes to make herself known to visitors when they least expect it, usually when they're busy working, participating in an activity, or trying to get some rest inside their tents or campers.

There are a number of campsites at Moon Lake, a natural, one-mile-long body of water about thirty miles north of Duchesne in the Ashley National Forest. The lake could have been named because of its crescent shape or for the round moon-like mountain on one side of it. Names aside, the lake is a gem to those who know about its raw beauty and the long, sandy beach that stretches the entire length of its western shore. Doug Robinson, in a June 15, 1989, article in the *Deseret News*, called the beach "a rarity in the Rock Mountains."

Little Vicki is a rarity, too, because even though she's been seen by a few and heard by even more, not everyone who visits the lake encounters the lost little ghost girl. Some who have heard moaning sounds believe them to be nothing more than wind.

The Moon Lake Monster

There's another story about Moon Lake that has circulated for much longer: the legend of the Moon Lake Monster. Tales about a large serpent that inhabits the waters started when it was discovered long ago that parts of the lake have no known bottom. Some people believe the lake has subterranean passages that go beneath the mountains to the Cache National Forest lake system, said Christina Bailey, a cultural anthropologist with the Ashley National Forest. Studies have been conducted, she said, and parts of the lake are reported to have no discernible bottom.

With such reports, it's easy to let minds wander as to what water monsters might haunt the lake's deep and dark recesses. Yet stories about the Moon Lake Monster seem to go beyond the imaginative. Some people claim to actually have seen a serpent-like creature break the water's surface.

In an unsigned article printed in my grandmother Dora Mae Weeks's self-published life history, the author describes what one might see at the lake:

> He [Gary Sutherland] said [in 1994] that the lake would be calm, even mirror-glassy with no wind or boats to create a wake. This would only occur in the morning or around dusk because, throughout the rest of the day, breezes would riffle the lake's surface, camouflaging any apparition of the monster. When it did appear, however, one would see a V-shaped ripple moving slowly but steadily through the center of the lake, usually coming from the north end and zigzagging but mostly running closer to the far shore. He said it would appear like a rounded object pushing water in front of itself, moving smoothly enough to create a ripple but not a breaking wave. . . . Then, one morning around mid-June, I saw it. I was drinking coffee at daybreak in the Moon Lake Lodge watching a mirror-glass lake come to light and there it was— exactly as Gary had described. I gazed long enough to realize this warranted a better look. I grabbed my binoculars and stepped down the back stairs outside the lodge. Sure enough, no wake. I walked toward the lake past the horseshoe and volleyball courts and stood up on a log near the flagpole. I focused the binoculars again on the apex of the V as it approached the near shore. The binoculars gave me clear enough sight to know this was no beaver. And I don't know of any fish species that schools in a goose-like V formation like that, either. . . . and it was the only thing moving on the lake. It zigged toward the far shore, not sharply, but rather at a wider-than-right angle from the direction it traveled as it neared me. As it headed away, I observed the apex from the back and could see nothing breaking the surface; only the rounded push of water at one point, seeming just below the surface. The point

looked the same, coming and going. After another couple of approaches and retreats toward and away from the shore, the ripple gradually disappeared downstream in the sun's brightening reflection on the lake.

Bailey said she's never seen such a monster, but that it's common knowledge in the area that such a creature might really exist. I heard the stories myself when I was a child, and once while fishing with my family from the lake's sandy shore, I imagined a Loch Ness Monster–type creature raising its serpent head from the water and staring at me. Something supernatural came upon me and I felt the water's pull, tempting me to walk into its coldness and be swallowed by the lake and its monstrous inhabitant. The chilling aloneness of such a vision disturbed me, and I cannot think of Moon Lake today without thinking of this very personal haunting.

That aside, the lake was a favorite destination for my California-based family who just about every summer would travel to Duchesne County to visit Grandma and Grandpa Weeks. Fishing was one of our favorite pastimes, and Moon Lake was always the destination. For anglers, however, it isn't the only lake in the vicinity. The rugged country that surrounds the lake is home to forty-three other lakes and thirty-eight streams that are filled with native rainbow, brown, cutthroat, and eastern brook trout and kokanee salmon.

If you cast a fishing line at Moon Lake, make sure that you keep your eyes peeled for large monster heads that bob in the distance or that peculiar V shape moving in the water.

Clinking Glasses, Dark Shades, and a Ghost Named Mary

Ralph was asleep in his bed when he felt a tap on his shoulder. He opened his eyes, and was startled to see his three-year-old brother standing next to his bed, staring at him.

"What is it?" Ralph asked.

His brother replied, "I'm cold."

Ralph pulled back the sheets and invited his brother to get into bed with him, where he'd be warm. Ralph moved over to make room for his brother, but felt something next to him under the covers. Upon closer examination he saw that his brother, sometime during the night, already had crawled into bed with him. Then who, or what, was standing next to his bed?

Ralph all of a sudden felt cold himself, not so much from the temperature but from fright. The apparition at his bedside, which appeared to look very much like his brother, continued to stand and stare at him, seeing through him.

"I wasn't dreaming," said Ralph, now in his thirties. "I was awake."

He didn't talk more with the apparition. He was too scared to do anything but stay frozen in his bed. Then the apparition, whatever it was, moved away. He watched it walk out of his bedroom and down the hallway, his brother still asleep next to him in the bed.

It was Ralph's first encounter with the paranormal, but not his last. The incident occurred in his childhood home, now razed, in South Salt Lake. Since then, Ralph has had several close encounters with the strange and unexplained. Some of them have happened in restaurants.

Ralph Staples and his wife, Janna, own Salt Lake City–based Steam Team 2, Inc. and specialize in cleaning restaurant ovens. Their clients range from chain establishments to privately owned ventures in Park City and across the Wasatch Front. They do most of their work after-hours, when the restaurants have closed. And it's at those times when they sometimes have experienced activity they can't explain.

Their most unnerving experience occurred in 2005 at a restaurant in Park City. The night started off like any other night. They divided up the work and set about on their tasks. And then:

"What?" Ralph asked.

"What do you mean, what? I didn't say anything," Janna said.

"You didn't call my name?"

"No, I didn't."

Maybe it was someone talking outside. They investigated, but found no one. It was the first strange thing to happen that night, a night that seemed to explode with paranormal activity.

They heard something, like glasses clinking. They walked to the kitchen, where they found the hung drinking glasses moving against each other, as if someone had brushed up against them. The first thing they thought was that they weren't alone.

"I grabbed a knife," Janna said. "We thought someone had come into the building." No one was supposed to be inside but them.

They began walking to various parts of the building to investigate, checking the rooms and hallways. And, to their surprise, they saw a shadow figure dart across a hallway, from one room to the next.

That was enough. The whole evening the couple had been rattled by strange noises, phantom voices, objects that had been moved, and now a shadow figure. They weren't getting much work done so, at a loss for what else to do, they called the police. The officers arrived and checked the building, staying with the couple while they finished cleaning.

Janna called the restaurant the next day. "I don't know if you guys know what's happening in your building," she told them, "but something strange is going on there." Apparently, others had known for a while about paranormal activity in the building.

The Staples don't know why there was so much unusual activity that one night. They had by that time been cleaning the restaurant for several years and had never experienced anything as dramatic as they did then. One rumor is that the ghost of a train conductor's wife has been seen in the restaurant, which is located on Main Street in downtown Park City. Mining and trains are a big part of the area's history. But why a ghostly wife, believed to be named Mary, would seek to frighten a pleasant working couple is not known. Maybe what happened that strange night was something else entirely, something that is yet unexplained.

The Staples, who said they've had a number of paranormal experiences in other restaurants and other places where they've cleaned, today are amateur ghost hunters, often teaming with other Utah groups to explore historic sites and old buildings. "After experiencing what we've experienced for so long," Janna said, "we became curious to see what's out there."

Curse of the Lost Rhoades Mine

Talented adventure writers have created plots around lost treasure. These escapist novels, whether they take place upon the high seas or in the arid deserts, allow us to journey with our fictional friends to places and adventures we might not otherwise ever experience. The swashbuckling yarns and thoughts of searching for hidden treasure spur the imagination, and we might wonder what we'd do with such riches if they ever were to be uncovered. Thoughts of riches in Utah have spurred the imagination ever since the pioneers arrived and they heard about lost treasure mines. "There could be a lost mine for every major canyon in the Wasatch [Mountains]," wrote Lynn Arave in a September 30, 2003, article in the *Deseret News*. "For example, Taylor Canyon, east of Ogden, supposedly has a lost gold mine, and bona fide abandoned mines are plentiful in Park City, Alta, Willard, and other areas."

The Lost Rhoades Mine is by far the most popular of these mines. As its name suggests, this mine's whereabouts are lost or unknown to most people. Though it is believed to be somewhere in the High Uintas, the story is largely considered a legend. In 1850s Utah, however, it was anything but to the select few who, with the permission of the Ute Indians, supposedly ventured to the treasure mine that is believed to house gold, jewelry, and other Spanish treasures from the Dominguez-Escalante explorations of 1776. At the request of Brigham Young, the Indians in 1852 made known the mine's whereabouts to a man named Thomas Rhoads.

In 1846, before Brigham Young set out on the now-famous pioneer trip west, Rhoads journeyed from the Midwest on an exploratory trip to the lands west of the Rockies; he overshot Utah and ended up in California that October, according to *Deseret News* writer Twila Van Leer. Instead of backtracking, he settled into life on the Pacific and went to work for John A. Sutter, who in 1849 became tremendously wealthy when gold was found at his mill. Rhoads built his own nest egg while working at Sutter's mill, and when he returned to Utah that same year at the request of Brigham Young, he was one of the territory's wealthiest men and surely the wealthiest man in the church. Three years later, in 1852, at the request of Young, Rhoads would again venture into the gold mines, but this time to a secret cache known only to the Indians. Wakara, the Ute's most famous chief, allegedly agreed to show Rhoads the mine as long as the gold was used only for church purposes. Rhoads agreed and the journey began. Rhoads allegedly made several trips to the secret mine, and in 1855 when he became too ill to complete the journey, his son Caleb took the same oath and traveled to the mines with an Indian guide. When Rhoads recovered, both father and son made frequent trips, each time retrieving treasures from the mine. Later, the tribe's chief successor, Chief Tabby, denied access.

Faithful to their promise, Thomas and Caleb Rhoads never revealed the whereabouts of the mine, which started the legend. Ever after, people have sought in vain to find the fabled mine. Why can't anyone seem to find it? It is believed there's an Indian curse upon the mine that prevents would-be trespassers from locating it.

Tooele Valley

ON THE OPPOSITE SIDE OF THE OQUIRRH MOUNTAINS FROM THE SALT Lake Valley sits Tooele County (pronounced too-WILL-uh) and the expansive deserts of northwestern Utah's Skull Valley. It's a bit of a stretch to get here from Salt Lake City, for you have to travel on a narrow stretch of Interstate 80 between the southern shores of the Great Salt Lake and the northern end of the Oquirrhs. In wintertime, there often is fog that crowds the roadway, making the journey a bit harrowing. But it's just the right atmosphere for a ghost story or two.

The Walking Dead

When you're there, standing on the crunchy white surface, it looks as if you're in the middle of a winter wonderland. But it feels as if you're in an oven—just one of the ironies of Utah's Bonneville Salt Flats.

The Bonneville Salt Flats, located west of the Great Salt Lake near the Utah-Nevada border, are known for the timed-speed races held every summer on the three-hundred-acre salt surface. Over the years, a number of speed records have been set on the flats by both cars and motorcycles—and by newfangled contraptions that look a little something like both. Scenes from popular theatrical movies, such as *Independence Day*, have been filmed here. The *Star Wars* series was not, but the desolate landscape reminds one of the movies' desert planet Tatooine.

The Great Salt Lake and its salt flats are remnants of ancient Lake Bonneville, which during the Pliocene Epoch covered about one-third of present-day Utah and parts of neighboring states. Traces of ancient shorelines, representing different levels of the receding lake, can still be seen today etched into the mountains that surround the flats. Mother Nature is still the caretaker of this impressive salt desert, for according to one website, a shallow pool of standing water floods the surface every winter; it evaporates as the weather warms while wind sandpapers the surface. This smooth terrain is what attracts thrill seekers who come here with their machines to try to break speed records.

Besides the racers and movie crews, the flats have remained inhospitable to most people. Mountain man Jim Bridger explored the area in 1824, but it wasn't until twenty-one years later, in 1845, that the flats were explored completely by John C. Fremont and his survey party.

In more recent years, the spirits of dead travelers, dressed in pioneer garb, have been seen walking on or near the flats. Others say they've seen spirits dressed in more modern-looking clothes. To put a date on when the deaths of these alleged spirits occurred would be pure speculation, but a starting point would be the 1800s, when pioneers and other travelers ventured through here. The scorching sun, made all the more hot by the blurry whiteness of the salty landscape, drove some of the travelers, many of them already sick or fatigued, to their deaths. The bodies of murder victims also have been found in the marshes or other places near the lake or its flats, according to the stories. The spirits of these dead persons are believed to haunt the desert flats.

When standing on the crispy flats, heat waves cause objects to shimmer in the distance. If you're here watching a race, the vehicles appear clear up close, but they blur as they tear down the strip, becoming but a grainy image. Those who have claimed to have seen spirits on the desert might want to consider the topic of mirages. But what about those who, traveling along Interstate 80 in their air-conditioned cars or at night when the temperatures dramatically drop, claim to see apparitions of dead people along the highway? Also, the flats are hottest during July and August, but sightings of apparitions have been reported in cooler months as well. Is this yet another irony of the Bonneville Salt Flats?

The Ghost Children at Mercur Cemetery

What's perhaps most creepy about the apparitions that seemingly make their appearance in Mercur Cemetery is that most of them are the spirits of children. Josh Bryant, who has seen the apparitions, says their feet are seen under the trees as if they were playing hide-and-seek.

It doesn't matter what time you come here, Bryant said, shadow figures have been seen both day and night. Ghost hunters have recorded voices, and people have smelled soap or perfume. Women have reported being touched, with scratches or red hand marks that show up on their arms afterward. Footsteps have been heard, as if visitors are being followed by unseen bodies. And some claim to have unnerving feelings while visiting the burial grounds.

What's more, a shaded rider and his steed have been seen, but more commonly heard, galloping across the cemetery. Bryant said he knows it sounds like something out of "The Legend of Sleepy Hollow," but a number of people have reported encountering the same phenomena.

The cemetery, located in Tooele County, is the eternal resting place for the miners who worked in the valley's Ophir and Treasure mines. "There were a lot of mining tragedies in the early 1800s in Utah," Bryant said, noting that many happened at those particular mines. The cemetery also has a number of graves for the families of miners, including children.

Haunts at the Ophir Mines

Like its biblical namesake, Ophir was a land of plenty to the people who long ago mined their wealth from its earthen recesses. Those people were first the Goshute Indians and, later, federal soldiers who were stationed in Utah.

By the late 1860s, commanding his soldiers wasn't the only thing on Gen. Patrick Connor's mind. He sent his soldiers to prospect the valley, and their first clues to wealth were the Goshute Indians, who had occupied the valley for centuries. The soldiers wondered where the Indians retrieved the silver to make all the fine jewelry they were wearing. They built trust with the Indians and eventually were showed the secret place: a canyon in the Oquirrh Mountains, a range that separates the Tooele and Salt Lake valleys.

The new prospectors first named the site East Canyon and before long the soldiers began small-scale mining. Not long afterward they struck gold—or more accurately, zinc, lead, and plenty of silver. Because of the plentiful supplies of these metals, they renamed the site Ophir, after the mines of King Solomon.

Connor organized the Ophir Mining District on August 6, 1870, and before long the canyon became one of the most productive mines in the Oquirrh Mountains. Miners from California and Nevada soon flocked to the area, uncovering their own pockets of wealth. It's estimated that between the years 1870 and 1900 more than $13 million worth of ore was extracted from the mines, turning Ophir into a hub that in its heyday was occupied by more than one thousand people.

Like all good things, though, the boom didn't last. By the turn of the century, the mines closed and the town dwindled. Even so, "small operators continued to hammer the ground, periodically making small strikes as they tried to revive past glory," according to a state history of the district.

The Ophir Historic District, about twenty-two miles south of Tooele in Ophir Canyon, has since been organized to keep a bit of the past alive. It is open every year from May to October, depending on the weather, and visitors can come and tour the mining town that isn't quite the ghost town you'd think it is. A number of buildings still stand and a small population claim residency in the once-promising town. And, according to some stories, a few ghosts reside here as well. Most of the stories are about the mines being haunted by those who once eked out a living in their dark recesses. An array of shadowy and misty figures, unearthly voices, and unnerving feelings of dread have been reported in the tunnels. Its mines are a favorite for ghost-hunting groups and other thrill seekers who've come here to try to interact with the dead. Some apparently claim to have been successful. Dark mists and voices, including calls for help, have been detected in the tunnels. As with all places when exploring for ghosts and history, be respectful and do not trespass onto private property.

Old Tooele Hospital

An old hospital-turned-haunted-house attraction is said to be more than a Halloween spook alley. The building, now known as Asylum 49, is believed by some to be haunted by the very real spirits of the former hospital's patients, who apparently for one reason or another never checked out.

It's not difficult to imagine why a former hospital might be haunted. Besides the hospital staff, the ones who spend the most time in the care facilities are the sick and dying. Many people have died at the Old Tooele Hospital. The building itself has an interesting history.

Over the years, the building was known as many things but always as a place to shelter and care for its occupants. It first was used as the home of Samuel F. Lee, who built the mansion-style house in 1873. Around 1913, it became a home for senior citizens. Locals often referred to the building as the county's "poor house." It didn't become known as a hospital until sometime shortly afterward, when the county decided it would be a good place for a care center. When a new hospital was built in 1953, the old hospital was reverted back to a senior citizens home.

In 2006, Kimm Anderson had the idea to turn it into a haunted attraction, perhaps fitting because of the many rumors of ghosts that have been reported here. The building is much talked-about in paranormal circles, though not everyone is convinced the place is haunted. Some believe the stories have been made up to bring attention to the haunted attraction. The Utah Ghost Organization is one group that has conducted investigations in the building. A high number of EVPs have been documented, the group claims, and pictures have been taken of apparitions, shadow figures, strange mists, and orbs. People have been known to have been scratched here, objects have been seen to move of their own volition. The Travel Channel's TV show *Ghost Adventures* filmed a segment in the hospital, claiming to have captured on a reel-to-reel recorder an unexplained child's voice and thermal fluctuations, supposedly of passing sprit energy.

Others in the same circle say there's not much paranormal activity at all that goes on in the building. Is the building really haunted? I don't know. I tried contacting Asylum 49 for comment about the alleged paranormal activity, but no one ever responded.

The New Area 51?

If there's any place in Utah, besides the Skinwalker Ranch in the northeastern part of the state, that's considered the most active UFO area, it might be Tooele County. There is perhaps a reason for this. The county is home to two large-scale government facilities: the Tooele Army Depot, a nuclear-waste facility; and Dugway Proving Ground, a biological and chemical weapons-testing facility. Both encompass vast areas of Utah's western desert. Because of the nature of the work conducted at the sites they are heavily guarded, and officials don't take lightly to anyone caught snooping nearby. Those who've watched from afar, though, have reported seeing strange lights in the sky and unidentified flying craft.

Throughout the history of the country's search for UFOs, there's always been some kind of connection to government facilities. The logical answer is that the government likely tests new aircraft and war weapons near these areas, and those who happen to witness something odd in the sky, something they can't identify, wonder if it is an alien spaceship.

The illogical answer, one that causes skeptics' eyebrows to raise in a questioning manner at those professing the belief, is that otherworldly beings visit these government sites for purposes beyond human reasoning. Maybe they're keeping an eye on our military progress? Or has the government found a way to communicate with those outside our earthly existence? Is the idea of UFOs that much different than alleged paranormal occurrences? Each person answers that for himself or herself, just as they answer the question about whether they believe in otherworldly aliens visiting this planet. And yet stories abound about people having seen things in the sky that they can't quite explain. (See the story "UFO over Grover" in the Southern Utah section of this book, wherein a movie director tells his very personal account of something strange he witnessed in the night sky one summer night; and "UFOs in Utah Valley" in the Utah Valley section of the book, in which residents report having seen unexplained phenomena on a winter's eve.)

A number of unidentified craft were reported by a number of witnesses almost monthly between April and July 2003 in nearby Magna, which sits on the opposite side of the Oquirrh Mountains, according to the website AlienDave.com. A wave of UFO sightings also were reported here in 1967. Other locations with a high number of reported UFO sightings include Salt Lake City and its many suburban cities, southern Utah, and the Roosevelt area where the Skinwalker Ranch is located. In fact, there's nary a place in the state that hasn't had some kind of report of strangeness in the sky.

As for Tooele, "Numerous UFOs have been seen and reported in and around Dugway," Dave Rosenfeld, president of the Utah UFO Hunters, wrote in an email to the *Deseret News*, which was published in an article called "Is Dugway's Expansion an Alien Concept?" in the paper's November 4, 2004, edition. The article went on to say that "Most of the disks, black triangles, orange spheres, flying wings, and manta-ray shapes must be military aircraft, he thinks. But Rosenfeld added that military aircraft can't account for 'all the unknowns seen in the area. It might be that our star visitors are keeping an eye on Dugway too!' He considers Dugway 'the new Area 51. And probably the new military spaceport.'"

Southern Utah

EACH REGION OF THE BEEHIVE STATE HAS ITS OWN IDENTITY. SOUTHERN Utah is perhaps best known for its scenic canyonlands and the distinctive red rock and sand in places like St. George. But desert is not all you'll find in Utah's warmest climate. Here there also are rough mountains, rushing rivers, wooded hills, and lush meadows. And amidst them all are plenty of ghosts and other strange phenomena. In this section you'll read about the phantoms of massacre victims who haunt a pretty valley, the colonial spirits who visited Mormon church president Wilford Woodruff, a movie director who witnessed a UFO, and the strange creatures that allegedly haunt a strange highway noted for its devilish name. There's more, of course, so read on.

UFO over Grover

It was a warm evening in August. The stillness was broken only by the sounds of children laughing as they jumped on the trampoline and the voices of the adults talking on the back porch. As the night darkened around them, up in the sky, a light that made no sound at all shone down out of a single cloud.

Kurt Hale, a movie director who's created such films as *The Singles Ward*, *The Home Teachers*, and *Church Ball*, claims that he's "a skeptic on a lot of fronts," but does not doubt what he saw on a summer's evening some years ago in southern Utah. Hale remembers the experience as though it were yesterday, though his sighting of a UFO happened in 2000. In a phone interview on April 25, 2011, Hale related his experience, explaining, "I don't know what it was, but at the same time I'm trying to put it in compartments in my mind of what it should or could have been and none of it fits."

It happened like this: Hale and his wife, along with an uncle and aunt, were sitting on the back porch of their family's home in Grover, a small community in southern Utah. Hale's grandparents had built the house, which sits on about four hundred acres, in 1968. Over the years, it's become a retreat for family to gather and visit. While cousins jumped on the nearby trampoline on the hot August night, the adults chatted and laughed. And then abruptly they were interrupted by the appearance of a bright light in the sky. It came out of nowhere, Hale said. One minute there was darkness, and the next there was a huge spotlight shining down from behind a single cloud.

It couldn't have been an airplane, he said. There was no sound, no vibration of any craft. They all talked, wondering and offering ideas about what it could be. The children looked on in astonishment. Remembering his camera, Hale ran into the house to retrieve it and then captured just a few seconds of the strange light before it blinked out, appearing to go back into the cloud.

"What was the weather like?" I asked. It was a clear night, he said, with few clouds and lots of stars. The light, whatever it was, stayed on for about two or three minutes before vanishing.

Asked what he thinks it was, he simply said it's "unidentified." He can't think of an explanation for it. He's disappointed with the footage he captured on video, saying it isn't very good film. "Everyone seems to have a lot of personal experiences with little evidence," he said. "And I fall into that category."

Hale said there've been reports from others in the area who say they also have seen strange lights over Grover, but he's never heard anyone else say they saw any sky lights on that night in August 2000. The lone witnesses appear to be Hale and his family.

"We all saw it together," he said. "I'm not going to be the guy who says there isn't anything out there, because I do believe there is. But what that stuff is, it's unexplainable based upon our finite understanding . . . things like crappy camera footage. I'm a believer that there's a lot out there that we don't know. Whether we're going to be overrun by some antagonist alien population is debatable, though."

The Ancient Spirits of Newspaper Rock

Like words on a broadsheet, Newspaper Rock is inscribed with news of the day. One catch: it's not our day that the inscriptions describe.

The inscriptions on Newspaper Rock State Historic Monument, a two-hundred-square-foot rock located near Canyonlands National Park in southeastern Utah, date back some fifteen hundred years; it is one of the best-preserved sites of ancient inscriptions in the Southwest. Unlike modern newsprint, which is filled with descriptive words and complemented by photographs, these ancient rock drawings, called petroglyphs, are all about the visual. If you were a child of the times, the wall perhaps would read like a storybook. The dense drawings include pictures of people, animals, and symbols, most of which are unknown or mysterious. There are even drawings of six-toed feet.

There's something haunting about seeing petroglyphs, as if the ancient writers, or artists, left something valuable behind, and truly they did. The "journalists" who left their mark here were many, from several different Native American cultures, including the Anasazi, Fremont, and Navajo tribes. It is rumored that their spirits still roam the ancient Indian site, keeping watch over their drawings. That ancient culture obviously left a message for us. What is it?

The Lonely Spirits of Grafton

It didn't take long after the pioneers arrived in Utah before Brigham Young charged the Latter-day Saints with establishing communities throughout the territory. Obedient to their prophet's call, church members took to the cause, some going north, others moving west, east, or south. Towns rose and others fell, whether by fate or misfortune. Grafton was such a place.

The historic Grafton known today in Washington County actually was the second such-named community in southern Utah. The first, which grew on the banks of the Virgin River, was abandoned after days of incessant rain in January 1862. The rain caused flooding that forced the residents to flee their community. They settled about a mile upstream in a place they called New Grafton. Not long after arriving, the pioneers built irrigation canals, thriving orchards, a post office, an adobe schoolhouse that also functioned as a church, and a number of log homes.

Though they were building a new community, the settlers could neither escape Mother Nature's mood swings nor Indian hostilities. Indian attacks became so problematic, in fact, that by 1866, residents temporarily evacuated to nearby Rockville. Some of the farmers returned daily to work in their fields, but it wasn't until 1868 that residents began to resettle in the area. Their efforts were short-lived, though, for not long afterward, another flood caused people to leave. Those who remained continued to farm the land, and by 1886, they had built a town hall and a new two-story adobe schoolhouse that doubled as a church. The river didn't stay its course, however, and caused more flooding in 1909. Ten years later the schoolhouse held its final class. Only three families remained by 1920, and in 1944, the last of its residents moved away. Grafton was now a ghost town, stripped of its human inhabitants. But not of its ghosts!

Visitors have reported hearing phantom footsteps on the creaky wooden floorboards of the remaining buildings, feeling warm breath on their faces, and sensing whisks of air passing by them. Some have reported seeing shadow figures or having feelings of being watched.

If you visit Grafton, which sits just south of Zion National Park in Washington County, you may not encounter a ghost. What you will definitely see are the very real remnants of the old town, including the schoolhouse, post office, and a few homes, preserved by the nonprofit Grafton Heritage Partnership Project. Spirits or not, this ghost town is worth a stop to better imagine in a very visual way what pioneer life might have been like in southern Utah.

The Devil's Highway

In 1984, NBC premiered the weekly television drama *Highway to Heaven*. The show was about an earthbound angel played by Michael Landon who was sent to help people along life's highway. At the same time in Utah, there was a very real highway that was known as the opposite of being anything heavenly. And the specters one might have encountered on this roadway, unlike Landon's TV character, were not known to help travelers.

U.S. Route 666 has been called "The Devil's Highway" or "The Highway to Hell," because of the Christian fundamentalist belief of 666 being the Number of the Beast, or of Satan. The highway was actually designated 666 in August 1926 because of it being the sixth spur along Route 66. It retained that number when U.S. 466 was dropped a few weeks later, according to the Federal Highway Administration. Route 666 served not only the Beehive State, but the Four Corners area that includes parts of Arizona, Colorado, New Mexico, and Utah. Over the years, it seems to have lived up to its nickname, because many car wrecks and fatalities that have occurred along the highway.

The route attracted the attention of popular entertainment and media outlets, including articles and cartoons in *USA Today*, *The Wall Street Journal*, and *The New Yorker* magazine. A 1998 edition of *The New Yorker*, for instance, published a cartoon of a sports car passing a sign that read Route 666; the driver and his passengers were depicted as horned demons. In 1979, the hard-rock band AC/DC released the song "Highway to Hell," and in 2001, Lions Gate Entertainment released the movie *Route 666*, starring Lou Diamond Phillips.

So what's in a name? Apparently a lot, if you ask some folks. It's been rumored that the ghosts of crash victims, otherworldly demons, and possessed yellow-eyed dogs haunt the highway and anyone who dares to travel on it in the dark of night. Because much of the road passes through historic Indian country, there is talk of skinwalkers or multi-dimensional shape-shifting creatures that may appear in the backseats of cars. If there's any truth to the stories, there's no wonder so many accidents occur here. Looking in your rearview mirror only to be confronted with a ghost is enough to startle anyone off the road.

"Triple 6 is evil. Everyone dies on that highway," a DUI offender told a state trooper, according to an August 4, 1990, article in *USA Today*. Another person blamed Satan for all the tragedy that has occurred on the route, because "the highway has the devil's name," reads an August 3, 1995, article in *The Wall Street Journal*.

The route still exists, but is known today as U.S. Route 491. This prompts the following question: Is the road still cursed even though its name has changed? Rumor says yes. Some believe the mark of the beast is already imprinted on the highway even though the number of fatalities has decreased over the years since the renumbering as a result of safety improvement projects.

Visions of the Dead

One of the more memorable characters in early Mormon and Utah history was Wilford Woodruff, who in the late 1800s served as the fourth president of the Church of Jesus Christ of Latter-day Saints. Woodruff joined the church on December 29, 1833, after Mormon apostles visited his farm in Rushland, New York. Stirred by the fire of the Mormon gospel, he thereafter became a powerful missionary and zealot for the cause, taking the gospel to the southern states, the Fox Islands off the coast of Maine, and to Europe. He became a church apostle in 1839, migrated with Brigham Young and other Latter-day Saints to the Salt Lake Valley in 1847, and became church president in 1889. He served in this capacity from April 7 of that year until his death on September 2, 1898.

A year after he became church president, Woodruff, because of increasing pressure from the U.S. government, drafted the "Manifesto" that abolished polygamy from the church. Thereafter, any persons found practicing polygamy were excommunicated from the faith.

Woodruff was a devoted journal writer, having kept a record from when he first joined the church to his death sixty-five years later. He recorded not only his own activities but many historic events important to the church. If it weren't for Woodruff, in fact, much of Mormon history would be lost. Woodruff was an exemplary and charismatic church leader, but perhaps ironically, he also was accident prone. In a number of entries in his journals, he writes about the mishaps that, if things had played worse, could have cut short his active life. He ultimately gave credit to a higher power for preserving him. Woodruff was many things, but he was basically a visionary—in the most literal sense of the word. He recorded a number of spiritual visions he received throughout his church service, including one wherein the country's Founding Fathers visited him to ask that he do their temple work for them.

Temples are important to Latter-day Saints for many reasons. They believe their temples are specially sanctioned and dedicated houses to God, wherein a man and woman may be married not only until death do them part, but for eternity. Other special "ordinances" are performed in temples, including proxy baptism. Mormons, who believe their gospel is the one restored or brought back to Earth after a period of global apostasy, believe that authorized church baptism is a necessity for people if they wish to be able to enter heaven in the afterlife. But there had been many people throughout the centuries who had never heard about Jesus Christ and many who died unbaptized. In short, Mormons use temples to perform proxy baptism for those who have died. They claim the rite was performed in biblical times, often quoting Paul: "Else what shall they do which are baptized for the dead, if the dead rise not at all? Why are they then baptized for the dead?" (1 Corinthians 15:29.) They believe the rite was lost, as was the proper authority to perform such ordinances, after the death of the early apostles, but that it was brought back in modern times through the instrumentality of Mormon founder Joseph Smith.

Woodruff claims that on August 21, 1877, George Washington, Thomas Jefferson, and other early American patriots visited him while he was inside the St. George Temple, an elegant white sandstone building that stands out against the red lava rock of St. George. According to Woodruff, these spirits wanted to know why the church had not yet done proxy baptism for them. The twenty-six-volume *Journal of Discourses*, which contains hundreds of sermons and other teachings from the early church leaders, records Woodruff's testimony:

> I will here say, before closing, that two weeks before I left St. George, the spirits of the dead gathered around me, wanting to know why we did not redeem them. Said they, "Have you had the use of the Endowment House for a number of years, and yet nothing has ever been done for us. We laid the foundation of the gov-

ernment you now enjoy, and we never apostatized from it, but we remained true to it and were faithful to God." These were the signers of the Declaration of Independence, and they waited on me for two days and two nights. I thought it very singular, that notwithstanding so much work had been done, and yet nothing had been done for them. The thought never entered my heart, from the fact, I suppose, that heretofore our minds were reaching after our more immediate friends and relatives. I straightway went into the baptismal font [in the temple] and called upon brother [John] McCallister to baptize me for the signers of the Declaration of Independence, and fifty other eminent men, making one hundred in all, including John Wesley, Columbus, and others. (19:229.)

"It was a very interesting day," Woodruff wrote in his journal on that date. "I felt thankful that we had the privilege and the power to administer for the worthy dead, especially for the signers of the Declaration of Independence, that inasmuch as they laid the foundation of our government, that we could do as much for them as they had done for us."

Malevolence at Frisco

"Hauntings," popular paranormal writer Troy Taylor observed in his book *Haunted Illinois*, "are believed to be created from violence and bloodshed." That, in a nutshell, explains Frisco. Frisco is of ill repute, according to the historic record. Murder and mayhem were common in the small mining community that now sits lonely and alone in present-day Beaver County, about fifteen miles from Milford. Eventually, the people went away. Like a skeletal town, all that remains are a few abandoned buildings, its charcoal kilns, and a cemetery. As do a few spirits.

Paranormal investigator Joshua Byrant said Frisco is perhaps the most ghost-heavy place he's visited in Utah. He recounts several odd experiences he's had at the place, including seeing a full-bodied apparition, having rocks thrown at him, and hearing the phantom laughter of children. What's more, one of the buildings, an old saloon now vacant for nearly a hundred years, often smells as if a party is going on inside. On those occasions, the scent of cigar smoke, chewing tobacco, and body odor is easily noticed, just as if you had walked into the saloon during its heyday. One time while

Bryant was inside the building with a friend, the friend became so nauseous at the apparent smell of body odor and liquor that he had to leave the building to vomit. "It was that strong," Byrant said. Later, they stepped back inside the building and the ghostly scents of a lively saloon were replaced by the more expected musty smell of old wood and dust.

Named after the San Francisco Mountains, Frisco was established as a mining town when lead and silver were discovered here in 1875. The Horn Silver Mine was established the following year, and before long "mining merchants and drifters came in by the hundreds," writes Stephen L. Carr in his book *The Historical Guide to Utah Ghost Towns*. This was both a boon and a burden.

"Because of the lack of water, the town 'needed' 23 saloons to wash down the dust," Carr writes. "With that kind of a start, Frisco was soon known as the wildest town in the Great Basin. Killings were commonplace and the 'meat wagon' made especially heavy hauls after payday."

Besides the saloons, the town had gambling dens and brothels. A railroad ran through town, bringing with it the seedy. Allegedly, a Nevada lawman was hired to clean up the town, giving its reckless residents an ultimatum: Leave the town or be shot. He supposedly killed six men his first day as town marshal.

"It has been said that this place was like Sodom and Gomorrah," Bryant said about the mining town. Despite its wanton abandon, it succeeded at least for a time as a productive mine. Within ten years the mine had produced some $54 million worth of product. It is estimated that more than six thousand people occupied the mining town between 1880 and 1885. The town began to die after an earthquake struck on February 12, 1885, collapsing the mine. The mine reopened within the year, but not on the same scale as before, and by the turn of the century, only five hundred people remained. The numbers kept dwindling until 1929, when Frisco was completely abandoned. Carr writes, "The mills and charcoal kilns were quiet." The kilns, still standing today, are listed in the National Register of Historic Places.

Unlike some places, Bryant believes that whatever is leftover at Frisco—whatever entities haunt the site—are not friendly. A friendly ghost, for instance, wouldn't throw rocks at you.

The Haunting of Lake Powell

The serene beauty of Lake Powell is just one reason why people enjoy coming to this popular recreation spot every year. The 186-mile-long lake, part of the Colorado River in Glen Canyon National Recreation Area, stretches across the Utah and Arizona border and offers about two thousand miles of shoreline and ninety-six major canyons, some of them fifteen to twenty miles long. With such an expansive site, you'd think there'd be plenty to do here. And you'd be right. People come to the lake for boating, camping, exploring, fishing, hiking, horseback riding, off-road riding, wakeboarding, and waterskiing. What they don't usually come for is to meet a ghost, but that's surprisingly what some people claim to have done while trying to get in some rest and relaxation.

When you consider the area's history, it's not difficult to imagine why visitors might have encounters with the strange and paranormal at Lake Powell. The geology of the place alone speaks volumes. The first inhabitants of the region were prehistoric tribes of Paleo-Indians. The Anasazis, who like many ancient cultures have mysteriously disappeared, inhabited the area about 200 B.C.; and later, from about 1050 A.D. to 1250 A.D., the Ancestral Puebloan culture lived here.

Others visited here long ago, including the Spanish priests Father Silvestre Velez de Escalante and Father Francisco Atanasio Dominguez, who in 1776 led the first documented journey through the area. Their route is today known as the "Crossing of the Father," and it lies several hundred feet under the waters of Lake Powell. The first formal expedition occurred in 1869, when Maj. John Wesley Powell led a team of ten men on a three-month, one thousand-mile journey down the Green and Colorado Rivers. In 1872, John D. Lee—infamous for his role in the 1857 Mountain Meadows Massacre—established a ferryboat service that carried travelers across the Colorado. The crossing is today known as Lees Ferry.

Lake Powell was created in 1963 following the construction of the Glen Canyon Dam. It took seventeen years for the canyon to fill to the high-water mark of thirty-seven hundred feet above sea level.

When visiting the area you can't help but notice the majestic rock formations that surround the lake and give it a Native American ambience. It is the Native American ghosts that are just as interesting, but a bit tougher to see. Mostly, visitors to the lake who claim encounters with the ghosts say they've heard them rather than seen them. It is not uncommon for people to report hearing phantom flute music carried on the wind, or the sounds of laughing and crying floating like waves across the shores. Some believe the spirits that linger here not only are those of Native Americans, but the victims of boat accidents and drownings that have occurred at the lake, of which there have been several over the years.

Mourning at Mountain Meadows

Long before horror befell New York City and the world in 2001, September 11 was marked by an episode of terrorism that occurred in a secluded valley in southern Utah called Mountain Meadows. Today, in this otherwise peaceful valley, where the wind brushes the tall prairie grass, there stands a monument listing the names of the victims of a bloody and senseless massacre. But the granite marker is only one memorial to the one hundred-plus men, women, and children who died here. Their phantom cries, carried on the wind, are another memorial.

September 1857: The Mormons weren't the only people who sought a better lifestyle by packing up their belongings and heading west. In the mid-1800s, thousands of emigrants, after loading their handcarts and wagons, set upon the Oregon Trail. Some headed to the Pacific Northwest, while others took alternate routes though Utah and on to Southern California. One company on their way to the Golden State was the Alexander Fancher and John Twitty Baker party, composed mostly of families from Arkansas. They were a peaceful lot, seeking to do only what others had done before them. Their plans changed drastically when they stopped to rest in the lush meadow in southern Utah.

A fanatical band of Mormons allegedly feared that the emigrants had ulterior motives for coming to Utah, perhaps to spy on them for the government, and they vowed they would not again be forced out of their homes as they had been in Missouri and Ohio. Brigham Young didn't help matters with his war rhetoric. At one time during this period of contention between the church and the government, he was quoted as saying, "I tell you, the Lord Almighty and the

Elders of Israel being our helpers, they shall not come to this territory. I will fight them and I will fight all hell."

In southern Utah, John D. Lee and others conspired in secret to commit mass murder, which goes against everything the church and good people everywhere believe: That all life is sacred. But there's no reasoning with warped minds. The group would invite the help of the Paiute Indians and together they slaughtered the emigrants. It didn't seem to bother the killers that the group consisted mostly of women and children. The planned attack was set to occur on September 7. The morning dawned quiet for the emigrants, who were sitting around eating a "breakfast of rabbit and quail" when "a shot rang out and one of the children toppled over," according to an account by survivor Sarah Baker. More shots followed in quick succession, and the shrieks of Indians emanated from a nearby ravine; a few minutes later seven men lay dead at the camp.

For the next five days the Baker-Fancher party huddled in the circle of their forty wagons trying to protect themselves from the onslaught of the Indians—and Mormons who had dressed like Indians—who surrounded them. Things weren't looking good for the emigrants. Food and water were running low; some of the party were sick. And then on September 11, a white flag appeared, and members of the Utah Territorial Militia approached. It appeared to the emigrants as if deliverance was near after all. But the militia members, including Lee, had hatched another plan to fulfill their evil deed of murder. They told the emigrants that to pacify the Indians they must give up their arms and submit to the militia. No harm would come to them, they were told. The militia members would lead them safely out of danger's way, first to Pinto and then to Cedar City. Word quickly spread through camp, and the emigrants, not knowing what else to do under the circumstances, put their trust in this group of Mormons, who at the time appeared as their saviors. They surrendered their arms. The emigrants then were told to separate into groups, the men into one group, the women and children in another.

In hindsight, the whole scenario has all the markings of a death trap, and surely it was. When the militia members had led the emigrants several yards from camp, the shout was given: "Halt!" And the slaughter commenced.

The plan was to kill everyone older than eight years, but during the frenzied slaughter several young children also were murdered. One report says that an Indian stabbed an infant while its mother held the baby in her arms. The horrific episode, one of the darkest in Mormon and Utah history, lasted only five minutes, but when it was over more than 120 men, women, and children lay dead and bloodied on the prairie, their bodies shot, hacked, slashed, or bludgeoned to death. It didn't matter that some had begged and pleaded for their lives; their answer was the slash of a knife or the discharge of a bullet. The seventeen children who were spared, those young enough to perhaps not remember the perpetrators of the ghastly crime, were gathered up and distributed to some of the area families.

They arrived at Jacob Hamblin's home that afternoon, blood-stained and crying. Some eighty years after the massacre, one of the child survivors, Sarah Frances Baker, who was only three on that dark September day in 1857, recalled, "But even when you're that young, you don't forget the horror of having your father gasp for breath and grow limp, while you have your arms around his neck, screaming with terror. . . . And you wouldn't forget it, either, if you saw your own mother topple over in the wagon beside you, with a big red splotch getting bigger and bigger on the front of her calico dress."

As for Lee, who became somewhat of a scapegoat for the massacre, he bragged for the first couple of weeks about his part in the killings, but then for the next twenty years denied having had anything to do with it. Such was the story of many of the men who participated in the slaughter. In 1872, then going by the name of Major Doyle, Lee opened a ferryboat crossing near present-day Lake Powell. He was executed by gunshot in 1877 for his part in the crime.

"The story of the most violent incident in the history of the America's overland trails remains among the West's most controversial historical subjects," writes historian Pat Bagley in his hallmark book *Blood of the Prophets*, "yet even students of the American West have nearly forgotten the event. Most Americans, including many Utahans, have never heard of it." Many other books, by authors more savvy than I, have tried to answer the questions of why the Mountain Meadows Massacre occurred. What led a band of Mormons, who subscribe to the belief that murder is a grave sin, to commit such an atrocious and bloody act? One cannot fathom the thoughts that run through twisted minds like those of John D. Lee, John Higbee, Nephi Johnson, and the other perpetrators of Utah's darkest deed. And, it should be asked, what role, if any, did Brigham Young play in the episode?

The LDS church has repeatedly denied that Brigham Young had anything to do with the massacre. Historians, relatives of the victims, and others can't seem to agree, believing that while Young likely did not order such an attack, he fueled animosity against outsiders with his war rhetoric. The Mormons had been persecuted and driven by mobs from state to state; witnessed the slaughter of their own people at Haun's Mill in Caldwell County, Missouri; and mourned the cold-blooded assassination of their own prophet, Joseph Smith, while he was imprisoned on false charges in Carthage, Illinois. When the Saints settled in Utah Territory, they vowed they would not be persecuted and driven from their homes again. Did such talk fuel the misunderstanding and vengeful thoughts of Lee and his partners in crime? It appears so.

The church doesn't like to talk much about this horrific episode, known to history as the Mountain Meadows Massacre. It knows it's a dark spot and talking about it does little to promote the goodwill of the church. Former church president Joseph Fielding Smith, however, denounced the crime as a "bloody and diabolical deed," and as the most "horrible and shocking crime ever perpetrated" in Utah. And surely it was.

No wonder, then, that the quiet meadow, made hallow by the blood spilt here, is the setting for frequent paranormal activity. As has been discussed in another part of this book, there are at least six different types of hauntings. One of them, a residual haunting, is a "recording" of a traumatic or violent act. The negative energy of the incident is imprinted in the atmosphere and, like any other audio or visual recording, is replayed over and over again. If ever there were prime ground for a residual haunting, the lonely dell where the slaughter of innocents took place is it.

How long after a traumatic event do residual hauntings occur? If Mountain Meadows is any indication, it is lengthy, for spirit-sensitive individuals who visit the meadow claim to hear the moaning of the massacred. Here in this haunted valley you can stand amidst the prairie grass and spirits and scarcely imagine the horrific episode. On one lonely monument is inscribed this epitaph:

VENGEANCE IS MINE: I WILL REPAY SAITH THE LORD.
HERE
120 MEN, WOMEN AND CHILDREN,
WERE MASSACRED IN COLD BLOOD,
IN SEPT., 1857.
THEY WERE FROM ARKANSAS.

Bibliography

Books and Articles

Arave, Lynn. "Mythical Beasts Lurk in 5 Utah Lakes." *Deseret News*, September 23, 2001.

———. "Does Bigfoot Roam while Gold Lies Hidden under Indian Maiden?" *Deseret News*, September 30, 2003.

Associated Press. "Local Resident Fell to His Death in Rock Canyon." *Deseret News*, October 11, 2006.

———. "Old Lehi Hospital Being Demolished." March 8, 2009.

Bagley, Will. *Blood of the Prophets: Brigham Young and the Massacre at Mountain Meadows*. Norman: University of Oklahoma Press, 2002.

Bauman, Joe. "Is Dugway's Expansion an Alien Concept?" *Deseret News*, November 4, 2004.

"Beast of a Highway: Does Asphalt Stretch Have Biblical Curse?" *Wall Street Journal*, August 3, 1995.

Black, Susan Easton, and Larry C. Porter, eds. *Lion of the Lord: Essays on the Life and Service of Brigham Young*. Salt Lake City: Deseret Book Company, 1995.

Boren, Kerry Ross, and Lisa Lee Boren. *The Gold of Carre-Shinob: The Final Chapter in the Mystery of the Lost Rhoades Mines, Seven Lost Cities, and Montezuma's Treasure*. Springville, UT: Cedar Fort, 1998.

Carr, Stephen L. *The Historical Guide to Utah Ghost Towns*. Salt Lake City: Western Epics, 1972.

Cartoon of demons, *The New Yorker*, February 23–March 2, 1998.

Denton, Sally. *American Massacre: The Tragedy at Mountain Meadows, September 1857*. New York: Vintage Books, 2003.

Dougherty, Joseph M. "DWR to Take Charge of Fish at Steed Pond." *Deseret News*, January 15, 2009.

Fleming, Paul. "Mall Ghost Walked Quietly and . . ." *Salt Lake Tribune*, October 18, 1999.

"Governor Dawson's Statement." *Deseret News,* January 22, 1862.

Guiley, Rosemary Ellen. *Haunted Salem: Strange Phenomena in the Witch City.* Mechanicsburg, PA: Stackpole Books, 2011.

Journal of Discourses. 26 vols. London: Latter-day Saints' Book Depot, 1854-1886.

Kelleher, Colm A., and George Knapp. *Hunt for the Skinwalker: Science Confronts the Unexplained at a Remote Ranch in Utah.* New York: Pocket Books, 2005.

Kennicott, Philip. "Ted Bundy's VW Goes on Display at D.C. Crime Museum, but Should It?" *Washington Post,* February 19, 2010.

Kermeen, Francis. *Ghost Encounters: True Stories of America's Haunted Inns and Hotels.* New York: Grand Central Publishing, 2002.

Koltko, Claire Ellen, Natalie Rose Ross, and Michael Marsh. *A Remarkable Life: Personal Experiences from the Journals of President Wilford Woodruff.* Springville, UT: Cedar Fort, 2006.

Maffly, Brian. "Child's Remains Finally Repatriated to Tribe." *Salt Lake Tribune,* July 6, 2009.

Moorman, Donald R., and Gene A. Sessions. *Camp Floyd and the Mormons: The Utah War.* Salt Lake City: University of Utah Press, 1992.

Norman, Michael, and Beth Scott. *Haunted America.* New York: Tor, 1994.

"Robber of the Dead." *Deseret News,* June 3, 1893.

Robinson, Doug. "Moon Lake—Unique Yet Little-Known." *Deseret News,* June 15, 1989.

Romrell, Lee T., and Sharon Romrell Staufenbeil. *From Mining Town to Ghost Town: A History of Garfield, Utah.* Rev. ed. Self-published, 2008.

Strand, Bert. "8 Hikers Spot Elusive 'Bigfoot' in High Uintas." *Standard-Examiner,* August 25, 1977.

Sullivan, Tim. "Space Invaders: Urban Explorers Hack into Utah's Subterranean Jungle." *Salt Lake City Weekly,* June 11, 2007.

"Shhh … Do You Hear Someone Weeping?" *Deseret News,* October 18, 2005.

Smith, Joseph. *History of the Church.* Salt Lake City: Deseret Book Company, 1980.

Taylor, Troy. *Haunted Illinois: Ghosts and Strange Phenomena of the Prairie State.* Mechanicsburg, PA: Stackpole Books, 2008.

Thiessen, Mark. "Bear Lake 'Monster' Sparks Debate, Revenue." Associated Press, July 11, 2004.

Thompson, Bonnie. *Folklore in the Bear Lake Valley.* Salt Lake City: Granite Publishing, 1972.

Van Leer, Twila. "The Lost Rhoads Mine." *Deseret News,* July 2, 1996.

Walker, Ronald R., Richard E. Turley Jr., and Glen M. Leonard. *Massacre at Mountain Meadows.* New York: Oxford University Press, 2008.

Warnock, Caleb. "Provo Residents Furious over Rock Canyon Quarry Proposal." *Daily Herald,* March 27, 2009.

Weeks, Dora Mae. *Sacred Memories of Dora Mae MacAfee Weeks.* Self-published, 2004.

Bibliography

Online Sources

"About us. What is This is the Place Heritage Park?" *This Is the Place Heritage Park*. www.thisistheplace.org/general_information/about_us.shtml. Retrieved February 1, 2011.

"American Fork." *Haunted Sites in North America*. http://hauntednorthamerica.webs.com/americanfork.htm. Retrieved January 16, 2011.

American Fork Canyon and the Alpine Loop Scenic Backway. www.fs.fed.us/r4/maps/brochures/amer_fork_alpine_loop.pdf.

Bear Lake Valley Convention and Visitors Bureau. www.bearlake.org/history.html.

"Blank-Faced Phantom." *Horrofind.com*. http://usersites.horrorfind.com/home/ghosts/hauntedus/blankface.htm. Retrieved August 8, 2011.

"Camp Floyd/Stagecoach Inn State Park and Museum." *Utah State Parks*. http://stateparks.utah.gov/parks/camp-floyd/about. Retrieved May 2011.

"City and County Building." *Welcome to Salt Lake City*. www.slcgov.com/info/ccbuilding/default.htm. Retrieved July 29, 2011.

"Clearfield Park of the Month—Steed Pond." *Clearfield City*, July 30, 2008. www.clearfieldcity.org/index.php?option = com_content&task = view&id = 460&Itemid = 322. Retrieved July 31, 2011.

"Denver & Rio Grande: Bingham, UT." *GhostDepot.com*. ghostdepot.com/rg/mainline/utah/bingham.htm. Retrieved May 29, 2011.

Dunning, Linda. "Highway to Hell: Mysteries of Route 666 Across Utah." *History and Hauntings of America: Haunted Utah*. www.prairieghosts.com/highway666.html. Retrieved March 29, 2011.

Guiley, Rosemary Ellen. "Reevaluating Orbs." *VisionaryLiving.com*. www.visionaryliving.com/2010/04/08/reevaluating-orbs. Retrieved June 2011.

———. "What Is a Haunting?" *VisionaryLiving.com*. www.visionaryliving.com/2008/09/05/what-is-a-haunting. Retrieved June 2011.

"Haunted Places in Utah." *The Shadowlands*. http://theshadowlands.net/places/utah.htm. Retrieved March 6, 2011.

"Hauntings of the Ben Lomond Hotel, The." *Haunted Places to Go*. www.haunted-places-to-go.com/ben-lomond-hotel.html. Retrieved February 23, 2011.

"Hauntings of the Old Tooele Hospital, The." *Haunted Places to Go*. www.haunted-places-to-go.com/old-tooele-hospital.html. Retrieved July 2011.

"Intermountain Indian School Photograph Collection, 1955-1970, P0327." *Utah State University*. http://library.usu.edu/specol/photoarchive/p0327.html. Retrieved April 2011.

"Kay's Cross: Somewhere in North Kaysville," *Utah Gothic: The Dark Heart of Zion*. www.utahgothic.com/tour/Kay%27s%20Cross.html. Retrieved June 2011.

"Markers and Monuments Database." *Utah State History.* http://history.utah.gov/apps/markers/detailed_results.php?markerid = 2590. Retrieved January 20, 2010.

"Ophir Mining District (Utah)." *Utah State Archives.* www.archives.state.ut.us/research/agencyhistories/3135.html. Retrieved May 2011.

"Religion and the Paranormal." *National Study of Youth and Religion.* www.youthandreligion.org/node/39. Retrieved August 7, 2011.

"Rio Grande Railroad Depot." *HauntedHouses.com.* www.hauntedhouses.com/states/ut/rio_grande_railroad.cfm. Retrieved March 9, 2011.

Roberts, Richard. "Ogden," *Utah History Encyclopedia.* www.media.utah.edu/UHE/o/OGDEN.html. Retrieved July 2011.

Rock Canyon. www.rockcanyonutah.com. Retrieved April 17, 2011.

"Six Types of Hauntings." *Paranormal Daily News.* http://paranormaldailynews.com/2009/12/04/six-types-of-hauntings. Retrieved August 8, 2011.

"Strange Lights Appear in the Sky above Utah County." *ABC4,* January 27, 2011. www.abc4.com/content/about_4/bios/story/Strange-lights-appear-in-the-sky-above-Utah-County/Wo5f7K0sTEi6_tM5q_-hxg.cspx.

Symes, Steven. "Old Mill: The Most Haunted Site in Utah?" *Examiner.com,* August 12, 2009. www.examiner.com/paranormal-in-salt-lake-city/old-mill-the-most-haunted-site-utah. Retrieved July 2011.

Taylor, Troy. "The Phantoms of Dove Creek Camp, Near Golden Spike National Historic Site, Kelton, Utah." *History and Hauntings of America: Haunted Utah.* www.prairieghosts.com/dove.html. Retrieved July 2011.

"Utah." *U.S. Census Bureau.* http://quickfacts.census.gov/qfd/states/49000.html. Retrieved August 7, 2011.

"Utah Legends: Bear Lake Sea Monster." *Legends of America.* http://www.legendsofamerica.com/ut-bearlakemonster.html. Retrieved March 10, 2011.

Weingroff, Richard F. "U.S. 666: Beast of a Highway?" *U.S. Department of Transportation.* www.fhwa.dot.gov/infrastructure/us666.cfm. Retrieved March 29, 2011.

"White Lady of Spring Canyon." *Carbon County, Utah.* www.carbon-utgenweb.com/white.html. Retrieved July 14, 2001.

Acknowledgments

WRITING OFTEN IS A SOLITARY ENDEAVOR. RESEARCH AND PUBLICATION, however, are a group effort. There are many people who deserve my thanks in completing this book, including my editor Kyle R. Weaver. His expertise and guidance has been greatly appreciated, and Kyle has become a good friend—on Facebook and otherwise. Assistant editor Brett Keener helped streamline the production process, and artist Marc Radle created the illustrations for several of the stories.

Kevin Erickson, director and founder of the Cache Paranormal Research Group, and Joshua Bryant, a lead investigator with the group, have been most helpful in sharing information, photos, and stories. I especially thank Kevin for taking the time to personally show me some of northern Utah's haunted hot spots and for all of the invitations from the group to join them on investigations or at other events. Tresha Kramer, marketing director for This Is the Place Heritage Park, and historical interpreters "Diamond" Jim Davis and Kendra Babitz provided information and stories about the park.

Others who deserve my thanks include movie director Kurt Hale, of Hale Storm Entertainment; Christina Bailey, a cultural anthropologist with the Ashley National Forest; Shannon Giles, a ranger with the Ashley National Forest; Trish Hull, manager of the Magna Public Library; Mark Trotters, park manager of Camp Floyd/Stagecoach Inn; Blake Citte, manager of the Ben Lomond Hotel; Ralph and Janna Staples, owners of Steam Team 2; Troy and LeAnna Reardon, owners of the Union Stockyard Exchange building in Ogden; and Jennifer Doan of the Paranormal Investigations Team of Utah. I appreciate everyone who answered questions, responded to emails, or in other ways provided information, stories, and leads.

Family and friends who pointed me in directions that opened further research or sources include Craig Weeks, Keith Fleetwood, Caleb Weeks, Alicia Jackson, Linda Snyder, and Al Laney. Special thanks to my wife, Heidi, and our son Brayden, who motivated and encouraged me when I felt discouraged or unfocused. Thank you, Heidi, for your help with last-minute preparations of the manuscript. And to my mom, Vivian, thanks for believing in me and knowing this day would one day come.

Lastly, I appreciate the authors and journalists whose books, articles, and websites helped me in the research and writing of this book. As a fellow journalist, I know how thankless that work can be at times. Thank you for your contributions.

About the Author

ANDY WEEKS, A GRADUATE OF THE UNIVERSITY OF UTAH, IS AN AWARD-winning journalist whose work has appeared in a variety of newspapers and magazines, including *Fangoria* and *Wild West*.

Other Titles in the

Haunted Series